Creating
Culturally Considerate Schools

In fond memory of Richard Ashburner.

Creating Culturally Considerate Schools

Educating Without Bias

Kim L. Anderson | Bonnie M. Davis

CORWIN
A SAGE Company

FOR INFORMATION:

Corwin
A SAGE Company
2455 Teller Road
Thousand Oaks, California 91320
(800) 233-9936
www.corwin.com

SAGE Publications Ltd.
1 Oliver's Yard
55 City Road
London EC1Y 1SP
United Kingdom

SAGE Publications India Pvt. Ltd.
B 1/I 1 Mohan Cooperative Industrial Area
Mathura Road, New Delhi 110 044
India

SAGE Publications Asia-Pacific Pte. Ltd.
3 Church Street
#10-04 Samsung Hub
Singapore 049483

Acquisitions Editor: Dan Alpert
Associate Editor: Megan Bedell
Editorial Assistant: Sarah Bartlett
Production Editor: Cassandra Margaret Seibel
Typesetter: C&M Digitals (P) Ltd.
Proofreader: Susan Schon
Indexer: Kim L. Anderson
Cover Designer: Rose Storey
Permissions Editor: Karen Ehrmann

Printed in the United States of America.

Library of Congress Cataloging-in-Publication Data

Anderson, Kim L.

Creating culturally considerate schools : educating without bias / Kim L. Anderson, Bonnie M. Davis.

pages cm
Includes bibliographical references and index.

ISBN 978-1-4129-9624-2 (pbk.)

1. Multicultural education—United States. 2. Minorities—Education—United States. 3. School environment—United States. 4. Cultural pluralism—United States. I. Davis, Bonnie M. II. Title.

LC1099.3.A54 2012
370.1170973—dc23   2012008929

This book is printed on acid-free paper.

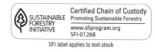

SFI label applies to text stock

12 13 14 15 16 10 9 8 7 6 5 4 3 2 1

Contents

Preface

This book has been writing itself as long as Bonnie and I have known one another. It has percolated as aromatically as the coffees we have shared over the past twelve years. We are very different women, yet we are united in our appreciation of things rich in flavor and fairness.

Creating Culturally Considerate Schools: Educating Without Bias blends the best of our individual work. Bonnie is a veteran educator and author with five titles to her credit and three more in the works. I am a veteran clinician and clinical educator with one title of which I am very proud and another in press. My contribution to this book begins with the phrase *culturally considerate,* a central theme of *Culturally Considerate School Counseling: Helping Without Bias,* published by Corwin in 2010. I am partial to this term because, for me, it opens the dialogue to include the parallel journey implicit in personal growth and professional development. Cultural *consideration* expands the notion of culture and allows for the variations within groups as well as between them.

As a result of my personal history, multidisciplinary training, and professional experience, I have come to use a very broad definition of culture. I value the importance of critical race theory, disability rights, and antipoverty initiatives, though make every attempt to avoid assumptions or prejudicial words that limit culture to issues of race and ethnicity, disability or socioeconomic status. Instead, I *consider* Heritage and Historic Memory, Geographic or Regional Origin, Circumstance and Situation, and Affinity or Relational Bonds. For me, this is the essence of intersectionality.

As I begin writing this book, forty-seven years have passed since Martin Luther King Jr. gave a speech at the Washington Monument sharing his dream for children. This week, Glenn Beck, with a dream of his own, rallied supporters to the same site. That is the beauty of our country. Two men with differing dreams can stand free in one place and share visions of a perfect world.

I see clients in a lovely office in an upwardly mobile part of the city. For most of my career, I had my own office. This is the first time I have sublet space in thirty years. Some of my clients have followed me from social service agencies to private practice. They do not always fit in with the décor of my current clinical space. I have been told that some of my clients "bother" other clients. I ask why. One day I was told one of my clients wore camouflage pants. I asked which one? I had two clients who wore camouflage pants that day. One was a mentally ill man who takes Medicaid transportation to my office from a rural county each week. The other was a petite woman who was delighted to show me the smart pair of camouflage leggings she found on sale at Neiman Marcus.

A single mom and her two teenage children move out of the apartment next door to me. They have lived there less than six months. She tells me the rent has been raised and it seems like very much to pay for a two-bedroom apartment. She is right. Two blond, blue-eyed university students move in a few weeks after Mrs. Lopez, Maria, and Jaime move out. I am saddened to think that we like our baseball players to be from Latin America but not our neighbors.

Each day I wonder what children make of events and incidences like these. Each day I wonder if an adult is correcting the misinformation or reinforcing it. What is that old sixties saying? *If you're not part of the solution, you're part of the problem.* I choose to be part of the solution. I assume if you have picked up this book, so do you.

Kim Anderson

From the Desk of Bonnie Davis

During workshops, I encounter teacher after teacher asking me how they can learn "what they don't know they don't know" about the populations of students they teach. These are well-meaning professionals who want answers and actions. I always suggest an inward journey: to learn what I don't know I don't know requires I look inside myself. Fortunately, in this book, I am able to both look inside myself, and at the same time, dialogue with a therapist about what I understand to be true. Hopefully, our reflective journeys in connection with Kim's reflective comments offer you, the reader, another method for examining our collective biases, expectations, hopes, and dreams for ourselves as educators and for our students as learners.

During my career, I taught English for 30 years in public schools; in addition, I taught in two homeless shelters, a runaway shelter for adolescents, a maximum security men's prison, and five colleges and universities. Since then I have been in hundreds of classrooms as a mentor, literacy coach, facilitator, and observer. Even though I have tons of classroom experience, I still do not know you, your staff members, or your students. I do not know your daily travails, joys, failures, and successes. But I do know so many places where I failed to do what I could have done to have created a classroom more culturally considerate for all students; at the same time, I know strategies I used that did create a culture of consideration. In essence, in this book you find descriptions of both failure and success, both daily travails and joys with suggestions for you as you work to create culturally considerate schools.

We call our work "culturally considerate" not because we believe you are not already practicing consideration of all students, but rather because we offer a framework for you to embed the work within as you examine your practice. This book is a guide, yet it is not a "should"—Kim and I present a framework for cultural consideration, and then you decide how to use it in your practice. One important difference between this book and my book of instructional strategies, *How to Teach Students Who Don't Look Like You: Culturally Relevant Teaching Strategies,* is that in this book there is a framework for taking action along with the bigger picture of why action is a necessity. We present the why along with the how. The why is the big picture, the research, the psychology behind the behaviors and the actions. The how is the implementation. If you are interested in learning the "why" of your classroom and your school, this book offers you scenarios for reflection upon the "why" of our actions as educators in a unique way that combines psychology and educational pedagogy. There are also research-based instructional strategies and numerous suggestions for embedding cultural consideration within your daily work. Finally, by using the framework, you will find ways to access and assess your capacity for culturally considerate leadership and instruction.

During the past decade, I have been consulting, presenting workshops, and providing coaching support to several school districts throughout the United States. In some districts, I have returned again and again to do ongoing, job-embedded work where I have had the opportunity to do research to test my hypotheses and practice culturally considerate strategies. Much of what you read in my writings in this book is based on the work in these districts. In these districts, I have had the opportunity to work with teachers in rural, suburban, and urban settings on an ongoing basis to support teachers in implementing culturally responsive instruction. I am grateful for the opportunity to share our journey with you.

Bonnie Davis

Acknowledgments

I am deeply grateful to our editor, Dan Alpert, for his unwavering support of this project. He never doubted the importance of the message nor our ability to present it. I am also grateful to our reviewers who embraced the material and gave us valuable feedback for sewing up a few frayed edges. Special thanks to Dorothy Kelly who reads with a wise eye and open heart.

I am most grateful to Bonnie Davis, my coauthor and coconspirator. Bonnie has been a source of inspiration and intrigue from the day we met in a mystery writing class some dozen years ago. I am proud to share this creative journey with her.

Finally, I am grateful to my family and friends who endure the obstacle-course floors and cluttered dining tables when the muse comes calling. I could not do this work without them.

~ kla ~

I echo Kim's words. I am grateful to Dan Alpert, a man who truly cares about the impact our books have on educators' minds and hearts. Dan always has time to listen, and he guides with a gentle heart and a keen intellect. My thanks to family and friends, especially to Dorothy Kelly who walks the book journeys with me both figuratively and literally as we stroll our neighborhood. Thanks to Kim, my friend and coauthor who refuses to limit others' potentials by categorizing and defining them and who continually offers me food for thought as uncomfortable as it may be, forcing me to continue my own journey. I wish to thank the administrators and teachers of the school districts where I have provided ongoing professional development during the past six years: Omaha Public Schools,

Omaha, NE; West Contra Costa Unified School District, Richmond, CA; Rockwood Public Schools, Eureka, MO; Kyrene Unified School District, Chandler, AZ; Chapel Hill-Carrboro City Schools, Chapel Hill, NC; Kirkwood School District, Kirkwood, MO; and Independent School District 196, Rosemount-Apple Valley-Egan Public Schools, Rosemount, MN. In addition, thanks to the organizations and districts who support my work.

~ bmd ~

Publisher's Acknowledgments

Corwin gratefully acknowledges the contributions of the following reviewers:

William A. Howe
State Title IX Coordinator/Civil Rights Compliance
CT State Department of Education
Bureau of Accountability & Improvement
Hartford, CT

Barbara Heuberger Rose
Associate Professor
Department of Teacher Education
Miami University
Oxford, OH

Tiffany S. Powell-Lambright
Assistant Professor
The SAGE Colleges
Graduate School of Education
Troy, NY

Deborah L. Misiag
Elementary Instructional Facilitator
Administrative Office of the Department of Special Education
The Old Cedar Lane School
Howard County Public School System, Howard County, MD

Ben Williams
Project Director
The Ohio STEM Equity Pipeline Project
Perkins Coordinator
Columbus State Community College

Richard Gomez
Coordinator, Educational Equity
Utah State Office of Education
Salt Lake City, UT

Maria Whittemore
FCPS Minority Achievement Coordinator
Frederick County Public Schools
191 South East Street
Frederick, MD

About the Authors

Kim L. Anderson's career path has been a diverse and divergent one. Prior to obtaining a graduate degree in social work from Washington University in St. Louis, she was a freelance writer, photographer, and graphic artist with interests in "outsider art," expressions of oppression and liberation beyond conventional artistic borders or boundaries. After many years of private practice as a licensed clinical social worker, clinical supervisor, and educator, Kim received a post-graduate certificate in art psychotherapy and now is a board certified art therapist. She is the author of *Culturally Considerate School Counseling: Helping Without Bias,* published by Corwin in 2010. Ms. Anderson presents her eclectic work at numerous local, regional, and national events and venues, engaging her audience through compelling narrative, careful research, evocative experiences, and instructive storytelling.

Bonnie M. Davis, PhD, is a veteran teacher of more than 30 years who is passionate about education. With a doctorate in English, she has taught English in secondary schools, community colleges, prisons, homeless shelters, and universities. The author of three Corwin books and numerous articles and book chapters, she is the recipient of many awards, including the World of Difference Community Service Award and the Governor's Award for Teaching Excellence. Davis presents annually at national conferences and provides services to school districts through her consulting firm, Educating for Change. Dr. Davis is the mother of two adult children, Leah Ancona and Reeve Davis, and grandmother of one granddaughter, Eva Salome Alvarez Davis.

PART I

Culturally Considerate Schools

1

Manner & Methods

Equity . . . multiculturalism . . . cultural proficiency . . . racial literacy . . . minority education . . . English language learners . . . achievement gap. These words fill the pages of professional development catalogs and continuing education programs, yet repeatedly educators say these terms have never fully been defined for them and ask *how* to employ these concepts in a real world, classroom setting. It is not uncommon for them to ask *why* they should employ such concepts. These individuals are sincere in their interest but equally sincere in their confusion. The sincerity of their words is unquestionable because the omission of cultural consideration, as evidenced by the startling disparity in student achievement between cultural groups, still exists.

While collegiate programs are graduating more and more diverse educators eager to close the gap which may have once interfered with their own school achievement, the majority of educators are still of the dominant culture. Despite the books and professional development resources available, few of them address the "whys and hows" of creating and maintaining a culturally considerate classroom, let alone suggest ways in which entire school environments can be transformed.

The heart of culturally considerate schools and promotion of cultural competence within administrative and student bodies is collaboration. Successful collaboration must be accomplished between like-minded individuals; disparate groups with conflicting agendas; and personnel whose heritage, history, circumstances, and affiliations are distinct and divergent from one another. With this in mind, we, the authors, offer a model for creating cultural equity, racial literacy, and diversity development but also hope to model collaboration throughout the text.

Self-awareness is the foundation for multicultural awareness and cultural competency (Saleebey, 1994). Many models exist in many forms and from different sources and disciplines. Geneva Gay (2001) writes, "As a concept, idea, or philosophy, multicultural education is a set of beliefs and explanations that recognizes and values the importance of ethnic and cultural diversity in shaping lifestyles, social experiences, personal identities, and educational opportunities of individuals, groups, and nations. Consequently, it has both descriptive and prescriptive dimensions" (p. 28). Christine Sleeter (2001) adds, "The great majority of critiques of multicultural education is that it is either too radical or too conservative" (p. 81).

Bennett (1993) suggests a model whereby cultural competence moves from *ethnocentric* stages of denial, defense, and minimization, to *ethno-relative* stages of acceptance, adaptation, and integration. Bennett's developmental model includes cognitive, affective, and behavioral components, as well as how the exercise of power manifests at each stage.

Ponterotto, Utsey, and Pedersen (2006) offer the Multicultural Counseling Knowledge and Awareness Scale, a 32-item, self-reporting inventory of perceived multicultural counseling knowledge and awareness which has undergone continued validation research. The authors caution that the instrument should be used only for research at this time and should not be used as an evaluative tool, though it is widely utilized in training programs and in some professional counseling settings.

Randall Lindsey (2004) has written extensively about the Cultural Proficiency Continuum, which describes a range of behaviors from destructiveness—the denial and suppression of a people's culture—to proficiency—the acknowledgment and elevation of all cultures. Lindsey, Roberts, and CampbellJones (2005) state that the behaviors identified on the continuum are not fixed, but rather descriptive points representing an array of practices and policies that characterize a developmental stage or phase of social competence (pp. 53–54).

The prolific Derald W. Sue and David Sue continue to present classic contributions to the field of multiculturalism, beginning in

1981 with *Counseling the Culturally Different* (1999). More recently, they have developed a Multidimensional Model for Developing Cultural Competence which integrates (1) the need to consider specific cultural worldviews associated with race, gender, and sexual orientation; (2) components of cultural competence such as awareness, knowledge, and skills; and (3) individual professional, organizational, and societal foci (Sue & Sue, 2008).

In 1993, James Banks conceptualized four approaches used to integrate "ethnic content" into elementary and high school curricula. Level 1, the Contributions Approach, focused on heroes/heroines, holidays, and food. Level 2, the Additive Approach, included content, concepts, and other additions to curricula without changing basic structure. In Level 3, the Transformational Approach, changes were made to the curricula which represented perspectives of diverse ethnic and cultural groups. Level 4, the Action Approach, empowered students to make decisions about important personal, social, and civic problems and take action to help solve them (Banks & McGee Banks, 2001).

Two other models are considered for direct practice implications in schools. First, "Multicultural Personality Development" from a "Strengths-Based" approach facilitates students' (a) understanding of themselves and their own worldviews and cultural biases, (b) knowledge of a multicultural history and of culturally diverse groups that they will likely encounter, and (c) skill development regarding interacting with culturally diverse individuals in new environments (Glassi & Akos, 2007; Ponterotto et al., 2006). Second, the Reflective Model of Intercultural Competency presents a multidimensional, qualitative data collection approach in order to evaluate college students' readiness for study abroad by assessing three dimensions of intercultural competency: cognitive, affective, and behavioral (Rundstrom Williams, 2009). This model reaches beyond community of origin and K–12 classrooms but transports cultural competency skills by reversing the roles of native and newcomer and might well find use in middle schools and high schools with highly diverse populations.

Add to these aforementioned models the venerable work of Gloria Ladson-Billings (1994), Geneva Gay (2010), and James and Cherry Ann Banks (2001), and one might wonder why another model, let alone a book, is a necessary addition to the literature.

We, the authors of this book, are schooled and experienced in complementary yet very different professions. Our mutual goal is to make education accessible and useful for every student and rewarding for every educator, school counselor, administrator, and adjunct staff member. As an educator, Bonnie is better prepared to share the *hows;* as a clinician, Kim is more about the *whys.*

Gibbons (2010) supports the idea that mental health objectives can sometimes be integrated with the needs and goals of the classroom and cites Camilleri (2007), who describes a classroom group protocol that provides the structure and limit setting that are important components for success when working with children experiencing environmental stress in the neighborhood and the classroom. Bickmore (1999) states, "The same elements that affect global conflicts are present in the elementary school." Conflicts are either interpersonal or intergroup and may involve bullying, anger, and violence in response to encounters with opposing viewpoints, needs, and desires of different people. By cooperatively identifying problems and their solutions, children can develop skills to succeed in the classroom and beyond (Hodges, 1995). But they need adults to help them build these skills.

In order to do this, adults themselves often need help in assessing, building, and utilizing their own skills. Bonnie and I offer *Creating Culturally Considerate Schools: Educating Without Bias* in an effort to provide a portion of that help and move beyond multicultural education of the 1990s by embracing the 21st century. In using "culturally considerate" classroom instruction, teachers will shift paradigms. They will expand their cultural lens as they infuse instruction with connections to students' life experiences, and they will more effectively respond to individual student needs using a variety of instructional strategies that cross cultures and content areas. This book contains teaching ideas designed to shift educator attitudes and encourages educators to *respectfully* interact with students, parents, and colleagues of differing cultures.

What to Expect

Creating Culturally Considerate Schools: Educating Without Bias is structured somewhere between a conversation between friends, consultation between colleagues, and a professional development workshop in print. We present our unique model of Cultural Consideration and Equity Skill Building, outlining the phases of personal and professional growth and describing steps to achieving them through research, narrative, anecdotes, and case example.

Research

In the process of collaboration, Bonnie and I discovered many things. Something we did not anticipate was how different our respective educations were in regard to research. Our academic backgrounds in writing and research were influenced by adherence to the MLA Handbook and the Chicago Manual of Style. In graduate school, Kim's programs required strict adherence to the Publication Manual of the American Psychological Association. Our publisher, Corwin, requests that authors utilize the APA style manual so we do our best but sometimes our writing reflects the basic intersectionality of our personal creativity and professional disciplines. Similarly, capitalization, punctuation, and grammatical constructions may sometimes differ, not only from the preferred Corwin style, but from one another. We retain them in order to maintain the integrity, individuality, and unique voice of each author or narrative subject.

Narrative Text

The task of facilitating this "workshop in print" fell to me (Kim), perhaps as an extension of my vocation as a facilitator and because of my relationship to the model content as a result of my previous book. I am an observer of human nature, a collector of experiences, and a storyteller who values oral tradition and the power of metaphor. Bonnie's narrative portions reveal her vast knowledge of student potential, classroom experience, writing elegance, and expertise as an educational consultant. She writes about how to do what needs to be done in clear and poignant passages.

In an article describing a four-phase pedagogical project they undertook to reduce pre-service educators' resistance to classes including discussions of race cognizance, white privilege, and social action, Gillespie, Ashbaugh, and DeFiore (2002) wrote, "Narrative methodology allows for the discovery of new meaning in past actions; these new meanings can then evoke new possibilities for future actions."

Vignettes, Anecdotes, Classroom and Case Examples

Throughout the book, Bonnie and I have used vignettes, anecdotes, and classroom/case examples to illustrate circumstances in which cultural consideration is absent, how our model applies to these circumstances, and what a culturally considerate school environment looks like. We agree with McLeod (2010) who asserts that case studies offer a form of *narrative knowing,* an efficient way of representing and analyzing *complexity;* generate knowledge-in-context; and are an essential tool for understanding practical *expertise in action* (p. 8).

In presenting these vignettes and examples, we follow the ethical principles of our respective credentialing professions (NEA, NASW, AATA, ATCB) and scholars McLeod (2010), Menkel-Meadow (2000), Sink (2010), and Sperry (2010). These principles are similarly outlined in APA Publication Manual guidelines which reflect two means of presenting confidential material: (1) obtaining written consent and (2) disguising aspects of the material by altering specific characteristics, limiting the description of specific details, and obfuscating case detail by adding extraneous material (American Psychological Association, 2001, pp. 8–9; 389).

Sperry and Pies (2010) prefer the development of composite case reports which construct a profile of a single, generic case by combining separate elements or characteristics from two or more clients/ situations in order to avoid accidental breach of ethical obligation. By blending features of more than one case, additional details may be added but individual identities and story lines are blurred. Composite case reports often have more pedagogical value than actual or disguised ones as material may be tailored to illustrate a theory, taxonomy, or treatment approach, are frequently safer alternatives to disguised ones due to the blending of separate characteristics of individuals, and ameliorates the practitioner's ability to obfuscate and protect client/student identity (Sperry & Pies, 2010).

Case-based evidence represents a form of practice-based evidence that has been central to the development of a balanced approach to social sciences education, combining both paradigmatic and narrative knowledge. No one form of knowing is better than another, but "human sense-making . . . requires both modalities to exist in creative interplay" (McLeod, 2010).

Frederic Reamer (2009) writes, "Case material brings ethics theories and concepts to life" (p. 2). Theories and concepts provide the conceptual guidance that professionals need to frame their assessments, program planning, interventions, and evaluations. Wrapping them around actual examples through anecdotes, vignettes, and case studies enriches practitioners' understanding and insights, providing a valuable lens through which to view and apply pertinent theories and concepts (p. 2).

Call to Action

Creating Culturally Considerate Schools: Educating Without Bias is finally a call to action. Throughout the book, we hope to inspire internal shifts in order to support external strategies for creating a culturally considerate school environment that

- Demonstrates awareness of the many cultures represented within the school community
- Gives voice and consideration to all students
- Welcomes all types of families
- Shows interest, empathy, and respect for each faculty and staff member
- Advocates respect and reverence of individuality
- Acknowledges limitations in resources and puts forth efforts to fill needs
- Admits mistakes and changes policy, programs, and personnel accordingly
- Adapts innovative policies in the interest of the total school community—even when uncomfortable or unpopular

As with Gillespie et al. (2002), who modeled for their students their experiences of power, privilege, and disenfranchisement, Bonnie and I endeavor to share our own experiences and emotional struggles to act justly and remain cognizant and culturally considerate. With cautions from these scholars, we anticipate "walking a fine line in challenging and engaging our readers, while not losing them altogether" (p. 245).

"Cultural consideration" allows for individuality and self-identity rather than assignment of labels by external sources. The model we present within this book was designed with the total school community in mind, the ultimate goal: success, achievement through equity. It is not a coincidence that it is a kinetic and progressive model. Less intentional, perhaps, is the inadvertent look at a diverse team in unified action. By engaging in interdisciplinary dialogue and discussion of differing styles, theoretic framework, and objectives, Bonnie and I also present examples of what can and does go wrong when cultural consideration is absent. To borrow a phrase, "what we don't know we don't know" *can* hurt us and our students.

2

Model of Cultural Consideration and Equity Skill Building

We, the authors, have built a personal friendship and professional affiliation upon examination of our individual pathways and converging corridors of cultural consciousness. In 2008, we searched the literature to find the perfect professional development model, but no one model suited the multiple purposes we had in mind, thus inspiring an eight-stage Model of Cultural Consideration and Equity Skill Building. The schemas on the following pages illustrate this model. Our model is kinetic and progressive, reflecting the authors' experiences and mutual belief that growth is a perpetual process and educating for change (Anderson & Davis, 2010) is an infinite responsibility. The first illustration depicts the developmental phases of professional growth. Self-examination, reflection, integration, and actualization culminate in educational equity. See Figure 2.1.

Self-examination requires an honest look inward as we explore, uncover, and reflect upon our personal views and how they impact our actions. Reflecting upon these views gives further understanding to how our thoughts, feelings, and beliefs shape our professional practice. This kind of courageous self-confrontation opens the door to integration of new knowledge and broader perspectives.

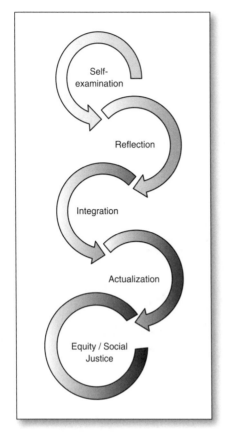

Self-examination

Reflection

Integration

Actualization

Equity / Social Justice

Figure 2.1 Phases of Professional Equity Development

Actualization occurs when we insert this knowledge into our work with the total school community. Educational equity exists when the principles of social justice are employed to improve and secure access for all students, parents, faculty, staff, and stakeholders. It is important to remember that a school without bias means that we, too, are supported, nourished, and nurtured in our work.

These phases of equity development are broken down into eight manageable stages of personal and professional growth: (1) Acknowledgment of Bias, (2) Assessment of Current Competency, (3) Acceptance of Limitations, (4) Cognitive Restructuring, (5) Expanding Knowledge Base, (6) Skill Building, (7) Culturally Considerate Education and Counseling, and (8) Reparation. See Figure 2.2.

After a combined 60 years of experience, the authors feel these phases and stages are essential to creating culturally considerate schools and achievement of educational equity. While numerous authorities include versions of these measurements, few underscore the necessity of the eighth stage—reparation—which both authors feel is particularly significant.

The delineated yet interconnected levels of the model are integral to understanding the holistic and evolutionary nature of equity skill building and attainment of social justice. The full model is depicted in Figure 2.3.

Creating and maintaining a culturally considerate school works for teachers because it provides the best possible learning atmosphere for the largest number of students and an inclusive environment for all kinds of teachers. If teachers and students feel things are working, schools are working. Creating and maintaining a culturally considerate school is best practice. It invites all students to share in the process of learning at their own pace and in their own way, sometimes in their own language.

Culturally considerate schools provide an avenue of access and achievement for all students. When students achieve academically, teachers shine. In this age of test scores and merit pay, it can also mean professional achievement for the teacher.

Describing challenges (of new teachers) in areas such as curriculum and lesson planning, assessment, management, time, and school culture, Feiman-Nemser (2003) and Agarwal, Epstein, Oppenheim, Oyler, and Sonu (2010) recognize that the current age of standardization and accountability significantly increases the demands and pressures for teachers in the classroom. Galman, Pica-Smith, and Rosenberger (2010) cite Bueller, Gere, Dallavis, and Havilland (2009) in suggesting that "by normalizing the fraughtness involved in preparing beginning teachers to become culturally competent, we can begin a conversation that will help beginning teachers and teacher educators alike embrace the challenges and complexity of culturally responsive teaching."

Geneva Gay (2010) defines culturally responsive teaching as "using the cultural characteristics, experiences, and perspectives of ethnically diverse students as conduits for teaching them more effectively" and asserts that when academic knowledge and skills are "situated within the lived experiences and frames of reference of students, they are more personally meaningful, have higher interest appeal, and are learned more easily and thoroughly."

Students instinctively know whether a teacher is comfortable in his or her own classroom or in his or her own skin. They also know whether he or she is comfortable with his or her own skin color or ethnicity, religion, abilities, or sexual orientation, and they respond accordingly. When a student sees, hears, or intuits that a teacher strives to be unbiased and considerate of his or her culture, he or she is more apt to not only *want* to learn, but *actually* learn (Anderson & Davis, 2010).

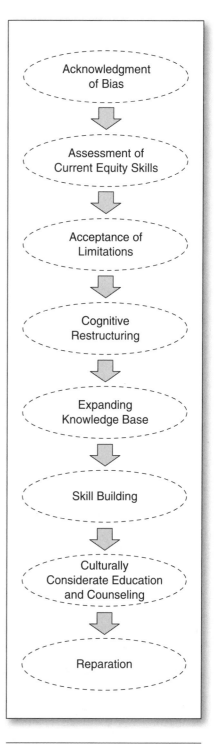

Figure 2.2 Stages of Personal and Professional Growth

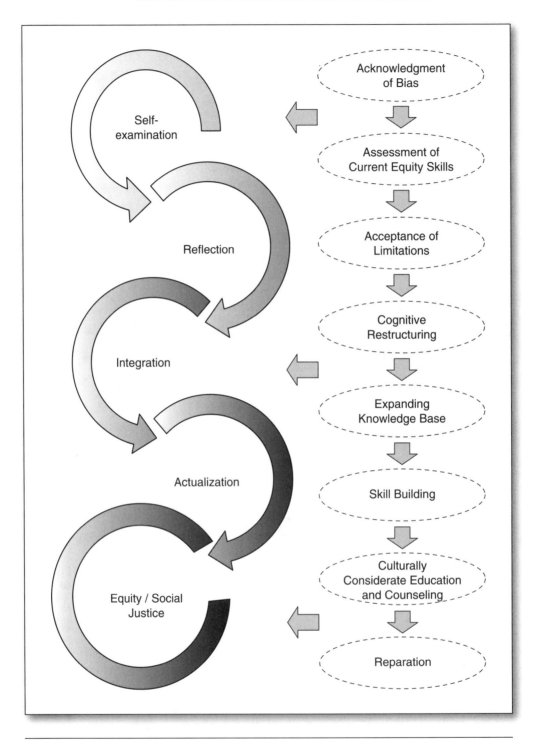

Figure 2.3   Model of Cultural Consideration and Equity Skill Building

Source: K. L. Anderson & B. M. Davis, 2008 & 2011.

Further, modeling culturally considerate and unbiased attitudes and behavior works for students because it helps them to learn by example. Drawing upon these examples, students develop social and critical thinking skills that expand their capacity to form relationships and problem solve with and among those who may look, act, and think differently from themselves.

We would like to say culturally considerate teaching is as easy as learning to swim but it isn't. For some, it may come as naturally as floating in a calm pool of water. For many, it requires overcoming fear and resisting the urge to fight the tide.

One of the requirements of my small, liberal arts college was that each graduate be able to swim. I grew up around creeks and streams, but I was afraid of pools and was not at all a natural swimmer. I thrashed about and exhausted myself class by class. One day I was too exhausted to thrash anymore and I stopped. When I stopped, I became buoyant. When I became buoyant, I could swim. So it is with learning new ways of being. When we stop struggling because of an irrational fear that we will succumb to some unknown undertow, we free ourselves of the biases and baggage that are likely to weigh us down and pull us under. Letting go of them releases us so that we no longer must grab hold and pull others down with us.

3

Practical Applications of the Model

Creating Culturally Considerate Schools: Educating Without Bias brings together Bonnie's insight as a classroom teacher and my intuitive practice as an expressive arts psychotherapist. We understand that in order for a school to achieve the goals outlined in the description of a culturally considerate school (see page 9), there must be a balance of practical "how-tos" backed by "why they work" for both classroom and professional development. The model we present ideally is applied and implemented at all levels. These levels include (1) Individual Educators, (2) Classrooms, (3) Professional Learning Communities (PLCs), (4) Administration, (5) Allied Professionals (school social workers, counselors, psychologists, nurses, etc.), and (6) Total School Communities.

Individual educators will have an opportunity to explore personal beliefs and values that may impact their professional practice, including suggestions for introspection and self-care, instructional and pedagogical strategies, and models for continued professional growth and development.

Classroom communities can be enhanced by the increased awareness and skill building of their individual educators. Students nurtured by sensitive teachers will naturally become culturally considerate individuals as a result of positive role modeling.

PLCs can flourish by using the book in study groups as a first step to becoming a more inclusive and open atmosphere for educators from all cultures to learn from one another. Strong and united PLCs can provide valuable suggestions and resources to administrators in order to create sturdy and culturally considerate school communities.

Administrators are urged to use the book as a professional development tool, not only for educators, but for administrators in an effort to model growth and professionalism which results in culturally considerate training and supervision.

Allied professionals can find themselves within the book as well, validating the valuable role they play in the welfare of students and school as a whole, yet challenging them to do their own work toward becoming more culturally considerate in their school counseling, social work, psychological, and nursing practices.

The total school community can and will be transformed if all stakeholders are involved in the journey toward equity through building a culturally considerate school environment. Students and their families, faculty, staff, administrators, and the surrounding school communities can be transformed by taking small steps toward a common goal.

Bonnie's Perspective

The Culturally Considerate Classroom is student-centered and honors every individual voice; in fact, it revels in individuality and difference. Difference is honored as an asset, and each student is taught to respect and learn from peers as well as the teacher. The teacher reinforces this respect of difference by continuing to monitor that she does not privilege one child or culture more than others, and she spends the needed time for reflection on her lessons, her behaviors in the school, and her continued learning of what she "doesn't know she doesn't know." She brings humility to the humanity in her classroom and continues her journey of cultural consideration.

Common Core State Standards

In June of 2010, the Common Core State Standards were released by the National Governors Association Center for Best Practices and the Council of Chief State School Officers. The stated purpose of the standards was to provide a consistent, clear understanding of what students are expected to learn, so teachers and parents know what they need to do to help them. The standards are designed to be robust and relevant to the real world, reflecting the knowledge and skills that our young people need for success in college and careers. With American students fully prepared for the future, our communities will be best positioned to compete successfully in the global economy. (Mission Statement, 2011)

The process of state adoption of the Common Core State Standards depends upon the laws of each state. Some states call for adoption through the state board of education, others through the state legislatures.

The standards are developed by the following criteria. They

- Are aligned with expectations for college and career success
- Are clear, so that educators and parents know what they need to do to help students learn
- Are consistent across all states, so that students are not taught to a lower standard just because of where they live
- Include both content and application of knowledge through high-order skills
- Build upon strengths and lessons of current state standards and standards of top-performing nations
- Are realistic for effective use in the classroom
- Are informed by other top performing countries so that all students are prepared to succeed in our global economy and society
- Evidence and research-based criteria have been set by states through their national organizations, CCSSO and the NGA Center.

Writing for the League of Women Voters, a nonpartisan, grass-roots organization since 1920, Janelle L. Rivers (2011) outlined the Common Core Standards and Assessments. She writes, "Students who move from one part of the United States to another during their K–12 school careers are likely to encounter substantial variations in curriculum. Standards for student performance vary widely by state." The strongest arguments against adopting the Common Core Standards for K–12 center on (1) the cost and difficulty of amending current curriculum and assessment tools, and (2) state sovereignty related to education issues (Rivers, 2011).

Forty-eight states and three U.S. territories supported the initiative, and the final report was passed on June 2, 2010. The U.S. Department of Education has not required adoption of the standards as a condition for federal funds, though states applying for grants associated with the Race to the Top program were required to adopt the Common Core Standards (U.S. Department of Education, 2010) which appears to have influenced the majority of states to commit to make the change.

Washington Post contributor Valerie Straus notes the connection to RTTT funds and cautions, "There are legitimate concerns about this [effort] and the notion that it is reasonable to ask every kid in every grade to know certain things. . . . The fact that few classroom teachers were involved in drafting the standards . . . makes me wonder" (2010). She quotes Diane Ravitch (2010) and Linda Darling-Hammond (2010), raising questions about focus of the standards upon quantifiable subjects and equitable access to valuable resources that ensure attainment of the standards for all kids in all circumstances.

Karen Effrem, MD, testified in front of the House K–12 Education Policy Committee in April of 2010. She expressed concerns not only about the Race to the Top funding, but that Title I funding would likely be in jeopardy when the ESEA was reauthorized if Common Core Standards were not adopted. Dr. Effrem stated, "The most serious problem with Common Core's ELA standards remains its organizational scheme. A set of generic, content-free, and culture-free skills do not serve as a basis for generating grade level academic standards" (2010).

Because we recognize the inevitability of the Common Core State Standards, we looked to the studies generated to review issues within the standards which might jeopardize cultural considerations in implementation. Several states reviewed the Common Core Standards in order to establish recommendations, among them, Pennsylvania, Alaska, Kansas, and Washington.

Pennsylvania stakeholders were broadly supportive of the Common Core Standards, though several roundtable participants expressed concerns regarding special needs and English Language Learners. Pennsylvania regulations now require all current teachers to receive professional development in working with ELL students and students who have special needs. In addition, Pennsylvania schools of education are required to incorporate similar instruction into their preparatory programs so that future educators will graduate prepared to meet the learning needs of an increasingly diverse student population (State Board of Education Academic Standards Committee, 2011).

Washington superintendent of public instruction commissioned a report entitled "Bias and Sensitivity Review of the Common Core State Standards in English Language Arts and Mathematics" (Relevant Strategies, 2011). This report was prepared as a result of a committee engaged by the office to review and offer recommendations to ensure the standards were implemented in a bias-free and culturally sensitive matter. A critical component of the review process was the initial committee orientation to the process and a review of current equity research and "opportunity to learn standards supporting diverse learners" (Lachat, 1999), as well as "transformative teaching and learning" through culturally responsive teaching (Banks & McGee Banks, 2009). In order to achieve optimum results, the committee directed that implementation of the Common Core Standards in Washington State must include intentional activities that support educators to

- Develop an awareness of and build upon the rich diversity of students' cultural backgrounds, family structures, learning styles, language and communication skills and patterns, proficiency levels, and methods of expressing ideas and operation as they develop instructional approaches, interaction groupings, classroom libraries, and assessment strategies;
- Foster exposure to and interactions with multicultural images, role models, and content which can support understanding, valuing and developing the craft, perspectives, and points of view of authors, mathematicians, and other practitioners from different background and cultures;
- Balance providing access to diverse, culturally rich texts, multimedia sources and cultural models with scaffolding learning activities to ensure that students acquire the requisite comprehension skills, cultural knowledge, and vocabulary to develop the CCSS for ELA and mathematics;
- Initiate regular classroom dialogue and other class activities to help students recognize, discuss, and address the emotional reactions students might have to bias in primary and secondary sources;
- Ensure access to technology and multimedia resources to provide culturally relevant and engaging materials while carefully selecting text, illustrations, and media to avoid biased or stereotypical representations;
- Give learners opportunities to develop and share their cultural heritage and personal stories and content knowledge and skills development and in their home languages, and ensure

equitable and adequate time to do so in response to their diverse needs and years of English language acquisition;

- Develop an understanding of the alignment of the CCSS throughout the kindergarten through high school progression in order to ensure that all learners are supported throughout their academic careers; and
- Use culturally responsive literacy and knowledge transfer strategies such as teacher modeling, discussion, charting, and graphic organizers to scaffold learning for students of differing abilities to increase their stamina, knowledge, and skills development.

In addition, the committee offered the following key recommendations to ensure successful implementation and ensure access:

- Equitable professional development based on professionals' skills and capacity;
- Professional development that engages and excites teachers and promotes collaboration and the intentional development of a growth mind-set;
- Increased participation of families, a strong community support network including mentors for learners, and alignment of teacher and family expectations and support for learners;
- The opportunity for teachers' input on curriculum and supplemental materials selection in order to distill high quality resources from among the large pools of available resources;
- Systemic diagnostic assessments and the right level of quality instruction between pre- and post-assessments; and
- Equal resources and equitable resources to address students' needs such as including an extended day, support for learners who move often, and ensuring that students who need special services do not miss out on basic education sessions (Relevant Strategies, 2011).

In *Opening the Common Core: How to Bring ALL Students to College and Career Readiness*, Carol Burris and Delia Garrity (2011) write, "It is not ours to decide who goes to college and who does not. It is our responsibility, instead, to prepare all of the students with whom we are entrusted to freely make choices. They can have that freedom if, and only if, we give them the skills and the knowledge that enables them to choose. If the Common Core State Standards stay true to this guiding principle, and not become ensnared in testing, then it will stay true to the principles of the Committee of Ten and their democratic ideals."

PART II

Model Phases

4

Self-Examination

Step One: Acknowledgment of Bias

Acknowledgment of bias is the first and most difficult step of becoming a culturally considerate educator and creating a culturally considerate school environment. Not unlike the twelve-step model of recovery, acknowledgment of one's addiction to biased beliefs and behaviors can be extremely painful. Awareness and acknowledgment usually don't happen on their own. No miracle occurs, no night-time apparition haunts us into revelation, but usually something does happen to force us to face our deficits. This something often falls into one of four categories: Personal Realization, Interpersonal Conflicts, Professional Crisis, and/or Unexpected Exposure to Social Injustice.

Personal realization may be silent, but is always profound. Examples of personal realization include a family member's

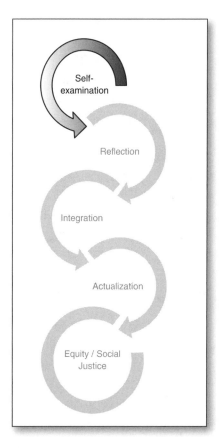

marriage to someone from another country, the birth of a biracial or multiracial grandchild, or discovering that a respected colleague is Muslim or a Republican. Realization that a change in mind-set and emotions must take place in order to sustain the relationship is often a profound experience and a decisive catalyst for embarking upon the journey toward cultural consideration.

Interpersonal conflicts may arise from any of these examples with immediate families, communities, between strangers, or they may arise at work between coworkers. Conflicts resulting from cultural differences, insensitivity, or disdain can be difficult to negotiate and resolve without both/all parties feeling the necessity to do so.

Professional crisis can occur when a solution to conflicts based in bias are so overt as to cause constant friction or fear in the workplace. Name calling, exclusion based upon race or culture, or refusal to confer with, work with, or hire persons of color, sexual minority, or alternate ability can result in sanctions, administrative leave, or even dismissal. At this stage, interventions are often too little too late and the individuals involved are abandoned in deference to the greater good.

Unexpected exposure to social injustice might begin with any of the previous examples but often ends with a personal understanding that something has to change. A sort of private revolution happens after a visceral response to an overt injustice such as witnessing an adult of privilege berate a child based solely on skin color or a family being turned away from a restaurant because the women are wearing traditional head coverings.

Bonnie writes about Acknowledgment of her own Biases

Acknowledgment of one's own biases is not fun. I can't say I enjoy the "A-ha" that comes with realizing my mind is filled with biases, prejudices, and stereotypes. Below I share some I am ashamed of in order to model for you the kinds of thinking one can examine when looking for Personal Realizations.

Writing this book, having conversations with Kim, and traveling around the country for work have caused me to examine the way I treat people.

Because my work has centered on African-American student achievement, I have continually reflected upon my behavior around and with African Americans, but I now realize I did not extend this reflection or cultural consideration to others. Part of this comes from my lack of familiarity in my daily life with people from cultures other than White, African American, and Latino/as. I have some book knowledge but not intimate family knowledge as I have with the mentioned three racial cultures. Another part of this stems from my being enamored by intelligence, power, money, and physical beauty. I'm ashamed to admit most of my definitions of these things stem from how society and the media define them.

What are some examples of when or how I might discount, judge, or under-value others?

Examples:

While watching a taxi pull up, I notice myself feeling glad that the driver is a "regular Black" guy. To me this means the driver is an African American, not a Man of Color from a foreign country, and I won't have to worry about not being able to understand his accent or confront him over taking a credit card. I feel terrible about this and think about what it means for those children or teachers who walk into my classrooms or workshops desiring to learn from me while I hold these preconceptions and biases about them. I reflect on how poor my accent in Spanish must sound to native speakers and realize I am insensitive and intolerant of others for things I am guilty of myself.

I fear being culturally inconsiderate to Asian people because I fear I will mistake one Asian culture for another and do something inappropriate. I have noticed this causes me to practice avoidance rather than learn what I don't know I don't know.

I find it difficult not to judge White people who misuse the English language. I have no issue with Ebonics or hearing some Black folks drop the past participle, but when White people do the same things and say "have went," it jars me, and I judge. Do I treat them differently because of that? I don't know, but I probably judge them as being less intelligent. At the same time, there are those I know who say "between you and I" which drives me crazy, too. And do I make grammatical errors—of course I do!

My 91-year-old father still comments he doesn't want to go certain places because they are all "old" people there; I take after my father. Even though I am legally a senior citizen, I struggle with my feelings when interacting with the elderly. I am not a patient person, and I need to slow down and be more tolerant of people as they age—just as I am aging!

Reflect upon your judgments of others. How do you combat these biases in order to practice cultural considerateness?

Questions/Reflections

❖ Reflect upon your judgments of others. What examples can you call to mind?
❖ Focus on one example. How might you turn the judgment into a culturally consideration of others?
❖ What "norms" might you develop in a classroom with your students to ensure no student judges another student inappropriately?
❖ Set a goal to alleviate negative judgments of others. Monitor your thought patterns and celebrate your successes.

Kim reflects . . .

Bonnie is hard on herself. Yes, she is my dear friend and respected colleague, but that is precisely why I can assert this knowledge. If she truly is as judgmental as she fears, we would not be friends or colleagues. This does not mean Bonnie is perfect in her attempt to be culturally considerate, but it does mean that she perpetually confronts and considers how she could improve her understanding of and relationships with people who are not like her. She and I have nearly brutally honest conversations about race and culture and aesthetic oppression. We agree on many things; we disagree on others. Regardless, we converse. We want to help make these kinds of conversations safe and productive for others, and therefore, throughout this book, we share and model some of our own conversations and thoughts about cultural consideration and conscientious practice.

Neither Bonnie nor I are without our biases or judgments but we are lifelong learners. Recently we had a conversation about the intersection between bias and boundaries. We talked about how a situation in which the sole Black woman at a school was "scary" to the white female educators, including Bonnie. Knowing how many of Bonnie's good friends are African American, I was unclear as to what she was referring. As we talked, it became clearer to both of us that the traits this woman demonstrated were not culturally based, but they were traits or behaviors that would intimidate most people. Confronting behavior and not culture makes it much easier to have a conversation which results in comfort for all. Negative behavior often results from rigidly holding or randomly blurring boundaries out of fear, anger, or ignorance *about* another's culture. Assuming someone's behavior is *because* of culture results in bias.

Recently I had a few moments of confusion regarding an uncovered bias of my own. A young client was discussing a former therapist.

I am quite fond of Sean, but in all honesty, he is a handful. I automatically assumed he had instigated the friction with his last therapist. I asked him to tell me what didn't work for him during the time he spent with Dr. Dreyfus.

"Well, I found it hard not to stare at his tongue ring," answered Sean who sports three tattoos on both forearms. I thought he was joking and I confess, I laughed heartily.

"I'm serious!" he boomed. "You try talking to somebody about usin' weed when they're sitting there with a mouth full of metal."

"You have a bit of body art of your own. I wonder why that was so distracting?" I asked, still suppressing a laugh.

"Yeah, but I'm not a doctor and don't get a hundred bucks an hour just to listen to people whine," Sean declared, then asked a surprising question. "Do *you* think that's professional?"

I managed to hedge answering Sean and refocus our conversation on his use of "weed," but I realized, no, I did not think that wearing a tongue ring during sessions was professional for a clinician. This caused me to ponder whether this was bias or boundary. As a clinical supervisor, how would I handle it if a supervisee showed up to see clients wearing a tongue ring? Should I handle it at all? I like to think of myself as open and pretty cool, but this cultural consideration confounded me. I generally have no problem with tattoos or piercing as I understand them in the context of the individual. For some clients it might be a signal of self-harm, for others, an expression of individuality, creativity, or allegiance. Apparently my understanding did not extend to therapists wearing tongue rings.

Another layer of this conundrum relates to my belief that the client (student) should always be more visible in the room than the therapist (educator), and a tongue ring, as Sean said, would likely be a distraction from the client/student. If this is true, what does that mean about my scars? Does this mean I should not practice therapy or present workshops because my physical body distracts from the body of knowledge I possess? Why do I think scars are acceptable but tongue rings are not?

These are questions I frankly am still pondering. My higher self knows that the answer lies in the conversation I would have with Dr. Dreyfus if I was his supervisor. It would begin in the form of a reflective question: *Have you ever considered how clients might react to your tongue ring?* But I admit I would be hoping he would not respond with the question I must be prepared to answer myself: *You ever consider how clients might react to your scars?*

Such are the questions we must all be prepared to ask and answer if we are to acknowledge our cultural insensitivity or intolerance. They are not always pretty or easy, but they are necessary if we are to truly confront our biases and maintain our boundaries. It might be suggested that there is a difference between scars and tongue rings because one is by choice, the other by necessity, but bias seldom knows the difference. Skin color, phenotypes, and country of origin are not choices either, but many people are biased each day by perceptions of race and ethnicity.

"Location of the self" is a process in which the clinician initiates a conversation about similarities and differences in their key identities. These identities include race, ethnicity, gender, socioeconomic circumstances, sexuality and spirituality, and how these facets of identity may influence (positively or negatively) the therapy/counseling process. "Implicit in this communication is the idea that these identities are meaningful and embedded in the work" (Watts-Jones, 2010).

In clinical terms, the "self of the therapist" refers to the personhood of the therapist as experienced *by* the client or as a vehicle of the therapy process by (voluntary or involuntary) action or active response *to* the client content. Both are mindful of the notion that a clinician's presence impacts the therapeutic process.

I am mindful of this in my clinical practice in much the same way I was as a young photographer after I read Susan Sontag's *On Photography* (1977). Our mere presence—as photographer, therapist, educator—influences those with whom we work. Our cultural identities and how they intersect are vital parts of our presence.

Kim shares her cultural biography

I define my culture of origin as Ozarkian. The culture of the Ozarks is generally misunderstood. Often the caricatures of Jed Clampett or the back-to-back cars lining the country music "Strip" in Branson are the first images that come to mind. Those are not my images. I hold images of honeysuckle and holly roses, clear streams, and craggy ravines sheltering deer and bobcats.

I am of Scotch, Irish, German, Swedish, and American Indian heritage. I am drawn to each. My maternal grandmother was the largest influence in my religious heritage, but she identified only as "Christian" and was not affiliated with any church. I was told to say we were Presbyterian when I was growing up because that was the religion of my father's family, but I'm not sure I was ever in a Presbyterian church.

When I was 6 weeks old, I was diagnosed with a condition called congenital hemangioma. While still a serious condition, it would be treated far differently today. In 1958, however, it was life threatening, the treatment was experimental. My surgeons made medical history, and my case was in text books and medical journals. Next to life or death, scars aren't so bad. Since I have had them all of my cognizant life, they, too, are part of my cultural biography.

In addition to my aesthetic considerations, my interest in cultural clarity likely springs from frequent moves throughout my childhood. My father worked for a large firm that built hydro electrical power plants and dams across the United States and overseas. We relocated often. I went to eight different schools in my first eight years of school. I became quite adept at sizing up my new environment, but I was also blessed by the constant of my parents' families in the mountains of southern Missouri, my culture of origin, rich with the twang of oral tradition and homemade fiddles.

The expanse of landscape and lifestyles of the various American small towns in which we lived intrigued me. The Indian reservation of Arizona, the military base of California, and the Mennonite community of Oklahoma all gave me a glimpse of the varied cultures nestled in my own country. As we moved from place to place, I took note of the Navajo women and children selling colorful woven blankets on the side of a dusty desert road contrasted with the Mennonite mothers selling quilts against pristine green pastures on Saturday mornings in the Midwest. Both spoke unfamiliar languages within their families. Navajo women were rarely disobeyed when speaking their native language. Mennonite women rarely spoke at all, but when they did it was often through the eldest son in quiet Germanic words. I remember wanting to stay longer and learn. I remember feeling a familiarity with such communities. Something to do with golden silence and order, colorful patterns and predictability. Above all, clarity. Cultural clarity.

Our family's perpetual moves stopped when I entered junior high school. My mother wanted to be near her family and thought I needed more stability in my teens. My father turned to teaching, an intention of his many years before. My interest in exploring difference turned to advocating for the different. At 16, I became politicized by the Vietnam War, the women's movement, and the aftermath of Watergate. While I believe our professions are often deeply rooted in our personal experiences and inclinations, I did not see clinical work in my vocational future. Unlike Bonnie, I saw myself more the social activist than personal advocate. I viewed injustice on a macro level rather than allowing myself to contemplate micro maladies. I now realize that my personal history made that difficult for many years. I needed to get my own psychological house in order before I tinkered with anyone else's.

My bachelor's degree was obtained at a small, private Christian college with which I'm still too angry to acknowledge. At the time, this was economic necessity stemming from my parents' divorce. While there, I witnessed religious hypocrisy, gender discrimination, homophobia, and the results of a widespread sexual abuse scandal on campus not unlike that of Penn State today. But I also received a good education in writing, photography, and graphic arts. I became interested in "outsider art," the art of those outside the normative culture, disenfranchised artists who spoke of inaccessibility and inequity through their creations, often looked down upon by those in the formal or established art community. I began to research artists who lived without boundaries or borders.

After college, I visited a friend who was in graduate school in St. Louis. While she was in class, I waited in the large social work library on the campus of Washington University. I began to explore the colossal collection of professional journals spanning topics from rural social work to women in media to multiculturalism. I had found my bliss.

Social work's mission is based on six core values: service, social justice, dignity and worth of the person, importance of human relationships, integrity, and competence. Social Work standards include "Ethical Responsibilities to the Broader Society" and in "explicit and forceful language" state social workers' obligation to address social justice issues, particularly to vulnerable, disadvantaged, oppressed, and exploited people and groups (Reamer, 2009). The personal and political became professional for me.

Along the way, I campaigned for the Equal Rights Amendment, I advocated for battered women in prison who killed in self-defense, trained by Lenore Walker. I interned and worked at a center for domestic violence and rape survivors. I initiated one of the first counseling groups for survivors of childhood sexual abuse, including one for lesbians, and advocated for interpreters so that Spanish-speaking and deaf women could receive services, relying on the expertise of people such as Suzanne Sgroi, Nicholas Growth, and Eliana Gil. I was trained as a systems family therapist in the styles of Virginia Satir and Salvador Minuchin and provided services to at-risk families and children in the most diverse neighborhoods of St. Louis. Finally, when I felt exhausted by the disregard for clients who were marginalized by agencies built on helping the marginalized, I left and with two other youthful therapists, started a group practice which later became a training program for counselors, social workers, and creative arts therapists. My professional culture has been shaped by experts such as James Masterson, Claudia Black, Terry Gorski, Christine Courtois, and Colin Ross.

And I have come "full circle" by completing a post-graduate program in expressive arts psychotherapy during which I trained with noted creative therapy mentors such as Cathy Moon, Shawn McNiff, and Pat Allen and alternative healers Michael Harner, Sandra Ingerman, Pat Tuholske, Louis Mehl-Medrona, and Lench Archuleta. In fact, my graduating thesis (2002) was entitled "Full Circle: Countertransference Containment through Mandala-Making (A Case Study of Closure)," and in it I wrote, "Thorough clinical work is predicated on therapist self-awareness and requires attunement and analysis," and quoted Christina Grof (1993) writing, "In the process of removing blocks that keep us from knowing our inner possibilities, we satisfy our intense thirst for wholeness" which in turn, allows us to recognize the wholeness of others.

Bonnie's Cultural Biography

Kim writes at the end of the chapter that students "don't need to know our histories but they will sense our unawareness of them." I agree they will sense our unawareness, but I also think we need to share our histories with our students. Just weeks ago, I observed a teacher sharing with his students how he grew up in their neighborhood, was homeless after his mother died, had joined a gang, and was given the opportunity to leave that life behind, enter college, and be their teacher today. The students connected with him through his history. My cultural history, or biography, is below. You may or may not connect with me through my history, but it does give you insight into why I passionately connect with the work Kim and I do.

A Cultural Biography focuses on those facts and experiences which form your cultural lens. The following is my Cultural Biography.

People often ask me how I, a White woman, became interested in race. The catalyst for my journey began on my 30th birthday in 1976 when I met a Black man who became my husband and the father of my son. Before that, my racial history consisted of White culture. Born in 1946 in an all-White area of southeast Missouri, my family practiced Catholicism and provided me with the idealized childhood of the 1950s. In third grade, I listened to a Divine Word Missionary speak of the work the church did in New Guinea to convert the population to Catholicism. From that moment on, I wanted nothing more than to be a missionary nun to New Guinea. I corresponded with nuns in New Guinea and kept my vocation at the forefront of my mind throughout elementary and high school. I entered the Sisters of the Holy Spirit at age 17, staying only a few months. This experience was devastating since I gave up a lifelong dream and suffered emotional consequences as a result of my convent experience. Eager to move on, I attended a local college and graduated with a major in English. At 20, I married and at 23 became the mother of a daughter who is one-eighth Cherokee Indian. In 1967, I began teaching in an all-White suburban district, and I taught for nearly a decade before the personal encounter with my future husband changed my focus in life.

I was superficially cognizant of race before. I attended the University of Mississippi (Ole Miss) in the 1960s and witnessed the segregation of people who did not look like me: for example, segregation at the university, at the Dairy Queen where the windows were marked "Colored Only" and "Whites Only," and at the dentist office. There were grocery lines where I was asked to "move ahead" of the "Colored" women who had been waiting before me in line. Rather than speak out, I simply accepted the protocols of the late '60s in the small Southern town of Oxford. I was in my early twenties, naïve, unaccustomed to being around anyone except Whites, and I am ashamed and embarrassed to say, I went along with the norm, rather than questioning the social and legal justice of what I saw around me. I wrote a thesis on William Faulkner, received an M.A. with honors, and was praised for my performance on my "orals," yet surely would have been given an F in social justice had grades been given for awareness of inequities and the courage to respond to them.

In 1984, the school district where I taught voluntarily desegregated, and the first Black students entered the schools. Since I was married to a Black man, the all-White staff assumed I possessed information about these students that others didn't; however, at the time I knew very little about Black culture or the home culture of these students. These students were largely ignored by the staff and other students, and one sympathetic teacher brought one of the students to me halfway through her first year at the school. She had written a letter to the school board informing them of the invisibility of the Black students. I read her letter and wept. For the first time, I paid attention to what was happening to these children at our high school and decided to form a club for students which we called The Organization for the Appreciation of Black Culture (OABC). This group of students taught me so much of what I didn't know I didn't know about students of color, culture, invisibility, and discrimination. At the same time, I found mentors and studied under folks such as Asa Hilliard and James Banks while reading the works of Geneva Gay, Belinda Williams, and Lisa Delpit. I traveled to the University of Senegal, West Africa, to study African literature.

I wrote a dissertation in which I investigated the impact of the dominant culture on the literary canon and the absence of women and people of color from that canon based on their nondominant place in society. I continued to learn what I "didn't know I didn't know."

Since the mid-'80s, I have facilitated professional development work in the area of equity for several organizations and institutions—as A World of Difference trainer for the Anti-Defamation League, a trainer for the Midwest Equity Center and the St. Louis Desegregation Office, and program planner for the Regional Professional Development Center (RPDC) housed at the University of Missouri-St. Louis where I supported and published the Action Research of teachers in the area of equity and instruction. Today I spend my time writing books and working as a presenter and equity coach in several school districts throughout the country.

In my personal life, I am a mother and the grandmother of a child of mixed ethnicity: Puerto Rican, Mexican, African American, and White. My daughter's husband of two years transitioned from male to female, bringing with it an entirely new set of learning experiences for me, as my daughter chose to stay married. My mother died. And life continues. After living more than 60 years, I have learned that each day brings more of "what I don't know I don't know" and that attempting to live life as a culturally considerate person is a daily learning challenge. Some days I do better.

―――――――――――――――ঌ――――――――――――――

Consider your Cultural Biography. Consider bulleting experiences that formed your Cultural Biography.

After having read the Cultural Biography above and bulleting your own Cultural Biography, what have you gained from doing this exercise as an exercise in Self-Reflection?

Step Two: Assessment of Current Equity Skills

Assessment of current equity skills is necessary to determine what has been driving our biases and resultant practices. Assessment of current competency begins with a tiny kernel of empathy. Understanding that others might feel differently than we do, have different experiences, or see things from a completely different perspective, requires empathy. Assessing our level of competency or our capacity for consideration of others necessitates we open ourselves to the possibility that we might not be attuned to how our behavior—born of our thoughts, attitudes, and beliefs—affects others.

There are many indices and scales to determine prejudice and cultural competency and schools can never have too many tools, though no source is more important than one's own heart and mind. Educators come to their work knowing how to size up school situations; yet, it is more difficult to dispassionately assess one's self. Assessment must include Thoughts, Beliefs and Attitudes and Behaviors/Actions. Beliefs are rarely proven to be true but are arrived at over time. Information, experience, and culture of origin reinforce beliefs. Because beliefs are difficult to prove, they are also difficult to *dis*prove. Attitudes are thoughts and beliefs manifested. Attitudes are conveyed through words, affect, mannerisms, carriage, dress, and environment. Words may be powerful, but these other expressions can announce attitudes at even higher volumes (Anderson 2010b).

Bonnie and I sat on my deck recently and discussed the impact of words. It was an early autumn day; in St. Louis, that means hot. The Midwest humidity is beginning to leave for the year and sitting outside at noon is tolerable, but it is still hot. In Missouri, autumn doesn't necessarily mean crisp and cool like it does in the Northeast—or even in Chicago for that matter. We were nibbling on various foods from the local organic grocer and writing this book. The impact of words—how different people respond in disparate ways to the same word—became an important anchor for this chapter. Autumn doesn't mean the same to everyone. Autumn is my favorite season, but not everyone has had a chance to experience the vibrant autumns of Washington State or Vermont.

Bonnie and I intended to combine the titles of our books. The title of her first bestseller, *How to Teach Students Who Don't Look Like You*, receives very positive feedback most of the time. It is accessible; it is honest; it is, above all, exactly what the book is about. The title of my book, *Culturally Considerate School Counseling: Helping Without Bias*, was not a difficult sell to my editor but received questions in the review process and caused some readers to feel offended after publication. I am curious about how words as innocuous as "culturally considerate" could offend anyone. I feel about this as I do about the word "empathy." When Justice Sotomayor was being confirmed, her use of the word "empathy" was called into question. How could she be impartial if she was empathic? My question is how can we be impartial—*unbiased*—if we are NOT empathic?

Knowing one's self entails *acknowledging* not just what one would like to know, but also what is difficult to know . . . including features we tend to project to others (Britzman, 2000). In his essay, *The Ghost in the School Room: A Primer on the Lessons of Shame*, John Tieman further asks that we consider the key psychological concepts of transference and countertransference and quotes Moore and Fine (1990, p. 196) in defining transference as the "displacement of patterns of feelings, thoughts, and behavior . . . onto another person," and states that the key to any successful interaction is the ability to endure tension without abandoning the interaction (Tieman, 2007).

Resistance as Change Agent

Bonnie describes her feelings on resistance

Kim writes about "Resistance as Change Agent." This is something I need to learn much more about since I don't do well with resistance. I like everybody to get along and agree. Yet I realize the power of resistance as Change Agent; this is an area where I need to work. When I walk into a group, I do not go in expecting resistance to the workshop. I work hard to establish a caring environment and lessen stress and threat. I walk around and attempt to meet each individual; I ask their names and something about them such as where and what they do in the district. I usually facilitate workshops that lead participants through examining their cultural lens and their classroom instruction. As I demonstrate strategies that work, I have them write down the strategies they observe, then we practice some throughout the workshop. I read the body language of the participants and monitor and adjust my presentation based on participants' responses. When the group is a volunteer group, they are usually engaged and demonstrate that through body language and participation. When the group is mandated to attend the workshop, engagement varies from group to group. My strategy then to meet their resistance is humor. Usually humor will soften their body language and create a space for learning. However, if the entire group is resistant due to their history or a particular incident that occurred prior to my entering the picture, I search for other ways to reach them.

Recently, I encountered a resistant group that happened to be a middle school staff. This is unusual because in my experience middle school teachers are easy to work with, having personalities that deal well with change due to the age of the children with whom they work. This is a generalization; yet this has been my experience. However, this middle school staff had a history and was resistant to the topic dealing with diversity. I tried humor; it didn't work. I tried empathy; it didn't work. It was only after I slowed down and decided to work on what they were interested in—themselves—that we made progress. I used an activity that defined for them their learning styles, and they related to it. They liked seeing their colleagues' styles as well as their own. Then I had them share their stories (personal biographies centering on issues of culture) in groups of five. After doing his, they returned to the workshop energized and behaving as a different group. Their responses to the group included such things as "it was really nice getting to learn something about Jane; I've worked with her for years and never knew her story." And "I liked hearing about all the similarities among us, yet I realized that our stories are so alike that we haven't experienced many different lens [sic] with which to see the world." The workshop that day ended not with a group hug, but it did end with the audience less resistant to future work. They individually agreed to implement a strategy and share back in a month how the implementation had gone. We did a final go-around in the room where every one of the 53 participants shared aloud what he or she planned to do. They left with a committed statement and homework to do. It works similarly in the classroom. By learning about each student as an individual and what each student is passionate about in his or her life, the teacher can begin with that passion and melt resistance in the student.

Reflections/Questions

❖ Think about where you encounter the most resistance. Why do you think it exists in those areas?
❖ What strategies have you developed to handle resistance to yourself or your ideas?
❖ In the classroom, what do you do to develop relationships with each individual student?
❖ How do you handle resistance in an individual student?
❖ What might you do differently in the future?

Kim responds . . .

Bonnie writes about resistance and describes walking into a room to do a presentation and being surprised when the audience is resistant immediately. Conversely, when I walk into a group, I expect and anticipate resistance. I am prepared for it. I even welcome it. For me, resistance gives energy to a room. It can be difficult, but I appreciate the challenge. I worry a bit when an audience is too engaged, too enthusiastic, or too positive. I don't trust it. In a group of more than five people, *someone* has to disagree with me.

In order to change, we often need something to push against (Einstein and Newton both had some notions about this)—not only because of the amount of energy needed to move mountains (or people) but also because folks generally need to feel it's worth their while to change. Resistance can be a measure of this worth.

When Resistance shows up, he may be late, but he's there and everyone knows it. Agreement arrives on time and with a smile. She doesn't want to bother anyone with her opinion.

What I find more alarming than either resistance or agreement, is Apathy. To me, Apathy is dangerous. Apathy is an invisible but deadly force—rather like carbon dioxide—the result of something potentially toxic. Resistance is difficult to move, but when it lets go, it gets things done. Agreement happily joins in to help. Apathy just sits in the way, watching while both good and bad things happen, refusing to take credit for either.

Whether we anticipate a calm classroom or an unruly and resistant group of our peers, there are some ways in which we can enter a room and set a safe and consistent tone. Bonnie and I established our rules of engagement when we were co-teaching a writing class for women. We share them here and write more about them on page 88.

Rules of Engagement

- Arrive Unencumbered
- Enter with Intent
- Attend to Self-Care
- Respect Others
- Circulate
- Ask Questions
- Leave Satisfied

These rules can also be found on page 138 of the appendix. These parameters came from our individual experiences as educator and group facilitator. They work well in most any circumstance, though you may want to edit and adapt them to fit the needs of your situation. If a school can adopt a consistent schoolwide practice of engagement, even better. Adults and students can all benefit when a positive and peaceable tone is set.

Pollock, Deckman, Mira, and Shalaby (2010) write, "Scholars have offered many important lists of the 'attitudes, knowledge, skills, and dispositions necessary to work effectively with a diverse student population,'" (Zeichner, 1992), but a recent review of research conducted for the American Educational Research Association makes clear that each teacher education program still proceeds with its own definition of the task. It is no wonder, then, that educators often express confusion about how exactly they should prepare to teach in a diverse and unequal nation."

Philomena Essed (1990) first named "everyday racism" as the re-creation of "structures of racial and ethnic inequality though situated practices" normalized as everyday life (Essed, 2002, pg. 192). Christine Sleeter states that preservice programs themselves provide disjointed multicultural content, dependent upon the individual professor and asserts, "By the time the student taught, they were concerned about surviving in the classroom. Those in primarily white schools had subordinated any interest in multicultural education to demands of their cooperating teachers. Those in urban schools were completely unprepared for the students and the setting and had great difficulty" (C. E. Sleeter, 2001).

Research suggests that many preservice efforts to prepare educators to teach in diverse settings pursue PD on race issues by asking educators to examine themselves personally in order to raise self-awareness of their racial biases, personal histories, privileges, and identities (Cochran-Smith, 2004). Similarly, according to Hollins and Guzman (2005), researchers studying efforts to prepare teachers for diversity predominantly seem to desire, expect, and measure personal changes in a teacher's mind (i.e., reduction in bias, an increase in awareness about privilege) and in a teacher's heart (i.e., a decrease in disdain for families of color or an increase in appreciation for urban schools for communities) more often than in the educator's observable practice. Far less research seems concerned with measuring what teachers are then able to do professionally for students, and even less research seems to measure actual interactions between teachers and students (Pollock et al., 2010).

Samuel Lucas (2008) argues that "teachers should inquire into students' individual lived experiences rather than use abstract notions about a . . . group to determine how students should be treated. Race, racism, and poverty conspire to affect teacher attitude, hiring practices, and social service delivery." Failure to acknowledge students' race or ethnicity in textbooks or school curricula disenfranchises minority youth in the school experience. The result may be that school is a child's first successes (Venson, 2008). "The self-view of the child of color is undermined when he [sic] realizes that the sole authority in the classroom—the teacher—feels that he is not as smart as White kids and isn't capable of catch up. Schools become a traumatic experience. While he wants out, his parents' insistence that he stays in school and does well so that he 'amounts to somebody' haunts him. Unfortunately, the longer he stays in school, the more certain he is that he won't end up 'amounting to somebody'" (Rutstein, 2001, p. 23).

Teachers and other providers may be unaware of their own biases and prejudices or the institutional racism or homophobia that pervades society. Consequently, they may unconsciously hold lower expectations for cultural minority students than for young people who come from more recognizable or acceptable home configurations (Hughes, Newkirk, and Stenhjem, 2010).

Rutstein (2001) suggests that educational leadership should engage in a united effort to adopt the teaching principles of successful schools like Harlem Prep in inner-city New York. These principles are:

1. Teachers believe that all human beings are fundamentally good.

2. Because teachers don't assume they know the capacity of students, they approach all students with high expectations. Sensing their teachers' attitudes, students try hard to succeed.

3. Teachers want to do everything they can to help their students excel. This genuine desire stimulates creative ways to reach and teach.

4. Teachers concentrate on helping students discover and develop their potentialities. By discovering their potential, students develop self-respect and self-worth. They are motivated to learn in order to develop what they have discovered.

5. By exposing their students to the realities underlying the principle of the oneness of humankind, teachers are able to strip away the effects of the shortsighted "four races" concept and introduce students to the reality of the close relationship of everything on our planet. By embracing this principle, students find themselves studying in the rarefied atmosphere of a family.

6. Teachers impress upon their students the importance of service to one's fellow human beings and to the community.

7. Teachers employ an interdisciplinary approach to teaching, which results in students developing a feeling and appreciation for the oneness and interrelatedness of all things.

8. Teachers stress cooperation instead of competition.

Additional solutions are proposed to address the challenge of what must be done to get to the point where education is a viable, life-giving experience for every student. First, [educators and other professionals should be provided] training on the oneness of humankind and the biological, anthropological, and genetic principles upon which this philosophy is predicated. Second, these professionals would benefit from training on the principle of unity in diversity, which involves both intercultural and multicultural education. Third, those working with youth, irrespective of racial or ethnic background, need to understand the concept of "white privilege" (McIntosh, 1988).

Thus it is when we confront our current levels of aptitude, abilities, and ultimately, our limitations. In the next section, we explore the harsh reality of limitations and ways in which to address and amend them. First, however, we offer considerations for the self-examination phase of our model.

Cultural Considerations for Self-Examination

- Keep a journal of your journey. Record daily interactions with others. Reflect upon your communication: your responses and your feelings. Private self-reflection is the most important factor in increasing insight and affecting personal change. If we are hesitant to listen to our own voice, it is difficult to be considerate of other's. The more we know about ourselves, the less we project onto others. Students benefit from educators who are open to self-exploration and who not only encourage but model self-reflection.

- Define the terms "culture" and "cultural consideration" for yourself. List five things that make you a culturally considerate teacher. List five improvements you already know you could make toward increasing your cultural consideration. Writing to our own prompts reflects we are working on a deeper level and beginning to understand *what we don't know we don't know* and better identify those things we *do* know in order to build upon them.

- Write your cultural history. Find a quiet spot; put on music that calms you; do not think ahead about what you will write; keyboard or write several pages without stopping or checking for sentence structure, punctuation, grammar, etc. Let it pour forth. You will not know where you are going; you will only get there. Free-range writing—foraging for words without artificial ingredients—allows for an unobstructed vision of both our starting point and our future goals. Becoming familiar with our own cultural history gives us greater comfort with the impact history or historic memory may have on our students. Until time travel is conquered, no one just "shows up" in the present. Students don't need to know our histories but they will sense our unawareness of them.

- Share your history with a person you respect. Read each other's histories. Allow each other ten minutes of uninterrupted time to share your story; do not allow the other person to interrupt or question anything. At the end of each of your stories, take the time to kindly talk and share with each other. Another option is to do this in groups of five with your family or colleagues. Follow the same procedure.
- Videotape yourself with your students. Analyze your body language. Pay attention to whether you are consistently engaging and open with all students or whether you need more personal space with some than others. Also take note of how students respond to you as well.

5

Reflection

Step Three: Acceptance of Limitations

Acceptance of limitations is humbling. We are forced to admit *what we don't know we don't know.* Bonnie stresses the importance of this in her books and in her presentations. Bonnie urges educators to accept that this enhances their competency and clears their cultural lens (2006). Students are asked to be open to learning new ways of thinking about old habits. So too must professionals be open to recognizing limitations.

Family therapist Dee Watts-Jones (2010) cites a number of scholars who critiqued the issue of hierarchy and power differentials between clinician and clients from various points of reference such as women's studies and feminist therapy, race and culture, and sexual orientation/gender identity (Brown, 1989; Goldner, 1988; Hirschman, 2006; hooks, 2004; Pinderhughes, 1989; Roth, 1989;

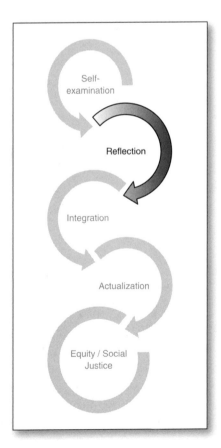

Waldegrave & Tamasese, 1993; Walker, 1992; Walters, Carter, Papp, & Silverstein, 1988).

Watts-Jones (2010) discusses the important subtleties of self-disclosure as it relates to self of the therapist. She states that self-disclosure ranges from factual matters of training and education, to personal identities and experiences. Used carefully, self-disclosure can strengthen the alliance between clinician and client and bridge gaps in social power between therapists engaged in cross-cultural counseling and therapy.

Earlier, I related a story about my client, Sean, and the importance of "location of self." Dee Watts-Jones (2010) writes,

> Learning to locate one's self requires a willingness to go into places that most of us still feel uneasy about engaging, inter-personally and personally . . . Practice, continued consultation, authenticity, and patience with stumbling are needed to achieve greater ease and quality in this process. Location of self also requires time.
>
> Location of self is about integrity in our work, a way of developing greater skill with addressing issues of inter-sectionality inside the therapy room, and demonstrating an awareness and interest in how issues of social status—those positioned as superior and inferior, and their respective entitlements and losses—operate in the lives of clients outside the room.
>
> For those struggling with their subjugated identities it can signal a welcoming that can validate their experience. For those with little recognition of their privilege and its relational impact, location of the self offers the message that these issues of relational injustice can be addressed to the benefit of relationships and the larger community.

Bonnie writes about Location of Self

As I think about what Kim says about the importance of "location of self," I real-ize I must continue to assess my equity skills and admit and accept my limita-tions in order to better understand my own location of self. I understand my cultural lens does not match the majority of young teachers and certainly not the students in today's classrooms. The following anecdote illustrates both my limitations and my attempts to assess my equity skills.

Recently during a workshop, I showed a video of two teachers instructing students. One was an African American woman and the other was a White woman. After viewing the video, the group had a heated discussion about their perceptions of the two teachers. Interestingly, some of the White women found the African American female teacher too direct and uninviting; the three African American educators and others (including me) found her to be warm and inviting. On the other hand, the White women liked the White young female teacher much better, even though she appeared to me to be much less inviting. Because this was a small group of educators, we could not make any definitive statements about our perceptions other than to voice that we cannot presume others share our perceptions.

In the late 1980s when I began presenting diversity workshops for The World of Difference, I had a missionary's zeal and believed I could change people's beliefs through my passion and presentation of research. I remember sharing Janice Hale's research on the learning styles of Black children (Hale-Benson & Hilliard, 1986) and being eviscerated by an African American counselor who said I was stereotyping Black children and that her son did not fit the research provided by Dr. Hale. I learned to become a better facilitator, and I moved further away from believing that I could find "the" answer and provide it to you to change your world. In fact, Dr. Barbara Woods, the director of the Afro-American Studies Department at St. Louis University, once said to me in private, "Bonnie, you need to do your diversity work with White people. Let Black people do their own work." At the time, I failed to understand her meaning, but as I continued to learn "what I don't know I don't know," I have learned to abandon the missionary zeal and to instead do the work on my own self. As an older, White female in this society, I have an abundance of work to do to rid my mind of my racist, sexist, classist, ageist, lookist, and all the other "ism's" I practice in my world. I understand I must continue to assess my equity skills and be willing to admit my limitations. One method for doing this is to have courageous conversations about these issues with my colleagues and friends.

Reflections/Questions

❖ What steps do you take to accept your limitations?
❖ In what venues do you practice equity skills?
❖ How do you assess your skills?
❖ What skills might you focus on in the future?

Kim adds . . .

When I train clinicians, I often talk about "narcissistic altruism," a term I use to describe what happens when the need to help a client—or in this instance, teach a student—blinds the helper or teacher and prevents him or her from not only helping the student but from progressing in his or her chosen field.

Many teachers and certainly the majority of school social workers and counselors chose their vocation as an outlet of altruism. Caring about others is a good thing. Helping others is a great thing. However, when one's professional identity is built solely upon these "good works" and personal identity is dependent upon them, a kind of narcissism comes into play. Sometimes this includes a misguided belief that no one else can teach or help as well: *No one else can understand this student as well as I can . . . I have more experience with this type of student or this population . . . I can handle this challenge because I'm tough.* All of these statements may be true to some extent, but they can lead to very costly mistakes for both student and teacher/helper.

The greatest risk of narcissistic altruism is recklessness. When we think we know it all, we are at greatest risk of not knowing what we don't know we don't know. As we have written about throughout this book and all others we have authored, knowing what we don't know we don't know is crucial to culturally considerate teaching. Remaining open and receptive is essential. This kind of self-absorbed and self-propelled compulsion to help has the potential to obscure our vision and muffle our hearing when we need them the most.

Gay (2002) urges us to understand that teachers have to "care so much about diverse students and their achievement that they accept nothing less than high-level success" but also warns that this is very different than the notion of "'gentle nurturing and altruistic concern' which can lead to benign neglect under the guise of letting students of color make their own way and move at their own pace."

As Lea (2004) found in implementing a portfolio approach to help white preservice teachers understand how cultural scripts shape their practices, such exercises cannot be effectively facilitated by white teacher educators who have not reflected on their own whiteness. This is true both as a prerequisite for the work and an exercise in modeling so that students will trust in their own process of struggle and risk. The same has been suggested in other accounts of innovative strategies (Marx, 2004). Cochran-Smith (2004) writes this is more than "making self-absorbed confessionals or baring one's soul to gain cathartic relief or public approval" (p. 13) but is instead a dialectical process of practice and reflection.

Gardner wrote about "the true teacher's defining affliction: 'furor to teach'" (1999, p. 93). He was referring to teaching in spite of students, maybe even *to* spite them (Tieman, 2007). Anna Freud (1930/1974), the daughter of one of the founding fathers of psychology, gave four lectures to teachers during her lifetime. She warned against blindness toward and defense against exploring one's interior life yet offered very particular frames for interpreting the dream of education including "rescue fantasies, altruistic surrender, hostility toward the student, and the difficulties of remembering one's own childhood researches." In other words, in order to teach, you must see the student, not just the subject.

A client I had seen in therapy for several years phoned one day and asked if she could come in for a few "refresher" sessions. When I had seen her last, she was finishing her graduate work and student teaching. When she came back to see me, she was in her fifth year of teaching. She liked her school, respected her principal, loved her fourth-grade students, but was beginning to have anxiety every morning before going to work. Much of our previous work together had been focused on her anxiety, and by the time she left therapy, she had made great progress. She hadn't had a panic attack for many years but was afraid if she didn't address the anxiety she felt, it would escalate.

After catching up on the past few years, we delved into the nature of her anxiety and how it was currently manifesting itself. Her eyes welled with tears as she began to talk. "I don't understand it. I really like my work. The kids are great. The people I work with are great. Everyday seems to be worse, though. I wake up. I start to get ready and the closer it gets to leave for work, the more knots I get in my stomach. One day my ears started ringing and I got dizzy. You remember. Almost like I used to do when I was student teaching."

"I remember. What do you remember about that time in your life?" I asked.

She laughed a little. "I remember I was a mess. I know I was scared of failing and that one boy made me feel like a failure every day."

I remembered she was a "mess," too. I also remembered that the boy reminded her of someone very important. I asked if she could recall why that student was so difficult.

"Oh yeah," she sighed. "I know he reminded me of Terry, my foster brother."

Terry had been one of several children her parents had fostered when she was young. His history was more severe than most of the other children, and he was a challenge for the family. My client, Courtney, had been a few years older. She was good with the other foster kids, but could never quite reach Terry. Eventually, her parents asked that he be placed elsewhere, but Courtney believed for many years it was her fault. She had often said, "If I had been better at teaching him how to act, he wouldn't have had to leave." The knowledge that Terry had committed suicide a couple of years later reinforced this feeling for Courtney.

I asked, "So who reminds you of Terry now?"

She looked puzzled. "I don't know. I can't think of anyone. Although there is a girl in my class who reminds me of me. She's the oldest in her family and has five younger siblings. Her mother brought them all in with her a few weeks ago when we had parent-teacher conferences. My student had to corral them all so I could talk with her mother."

"Do you think something about this student is causing anxiety?"

"I don't know why it would. I've been trying to find resources for her so she can better handle her little brothers and sisters; especially the one little guy who was running all over the place. Poor kid—my student—had to chase him down several times. I'm sure if she just had the right tools she could teach them all how to behave better."

I felt sad, hearing almost the same words I had heard her say years before. "Courtney, you know that's not her job."

She started to debate this with me. "But the mom is so overwhelmed and my student is a natural with kids. I'm sure she could do it."

"Maybe; but it still isn't her job. She's 10 years old," I reminded her.

"Yes, but I could do it at her age. Of course I didn't do such a good job with Terry . . ." her voice trailed off and she started crying. "*Oh no. That is it, isn't it?* I want to help her so she doesn't have to fail with her little brother like I failed Terry." She sobbed for a while then released a big sigh.

When she could make eye contact with me, I said, "You did not fail Terry. You were a child just like he was. Saving him was not your job, and saving this little girl is not really your job either. Especially if you are trying to teach her parenting skills at 10 years old."

"But what do I do?" she asked.

"What do you do for yourself or for your student?"

"My student. I'm not worried about me," Courtney said.

"The best thing you can do for your student is to take care of yourself. If you feel she needs something more, you can refer her to the school social worker or school counselor."

"So I really do need a refresher course on self-care, don't I?"

I heartily agreed with her and she did come in for a few weeks to "refresh" her self-care and anxiety reduction skills.

Courtney's experience is not uncommon. Many educators are faced daily with something that reminds them—consciously or unconsciously—of situations in their lives which produced strong feelings. Even when work has been done to alleviate the aftermath of these feelings, they don't necessarily "stay put." For anyone who works closely with them, the vulnerability of children is laden with the "rescue fantasies and altruistic surrender" to which Anna Freud referred. Like Courtney, recognition of limitations and focus upon unblocking barriers to self-care becomes the best way in which to help both educator and student.

Cultural Considerations for Reflection

- Collect moments in time when you notice a student's or colleague's culture. On an index card, write the name, date, and what you noticed. Reflect upon what brought this to your attention and write your very first thought after you noticed it. Now reflect upon whether you could share this thought with anyone else. Could you share it with the student or colleague?

- Make a list of the adjectives you use to describe your students. Put an asterisk beside words that would shame, humiliate, or embarrass you. Replace these words with neutral descriptors. Practice using them. Stark confrontation of our innate, second natures can be difficult, but acknowledging the words we use is an essential beginning. Becoming more culturally considerate starts with learning or becoming fluent in the language of cultural awareness. Words matter and students today take in words via a plethora of media. It is easy to think this numbs young people to labels or categories or descriptors, but in fact, it does the opposite as reports of school violence and student self-harm attest.

- Consider how you think and feel about some student's interests or characteristics. Perhaps you dislike rap or hip-hop or are suspicious of a student who wears a hijab or has an accent. Recognizing specific thoughts and feelings helps to identify biases. Learning about things with which we are uncomfortable helps to decrease and dispel them.

- Visit a large bookstore or go online and browse magazines or websites published for and by persons of a culture different from your own. Consider the headlines, story titles, or illustrations and compare them to similar publications you read on a regular basis. When giving assignments which involve current events and media, be sure to include some of these books and ask your students to reflect upon similarities and differences as well.

- Consider a situation involving someone from another culture that you might have handled better. Write the story from start to finish. Switch the race, gender, or ethnicity of the characters and read it out loud to yourself. Be conscious of how you think, feel, and what you believe as you play the role of the student or colleague. There is a distinct difference in intent and outcome. Educators seldom intend to be racist, sexist, or homophobic, but as products of a society that routinely harbors these "isms," we all make errors that affect our students. Viewing an interaction from another's point of view helps to gain perspective.

6

Integration

Step Four: Cognitive Restructuring

Cognitive restructuring is a primarily clinical term used in behavioral therapies but is applicable to many situations and comes from a variety of sources, most notably, Albert Ellis (1978) and Aaron T. Beck (1979). Cognitive restructuring replaces "faulty thinking" with thoughts derived from accurate information and fundamental understanding of the issue or situation at hand. While this is important, it is relatively useless unless these new thoughts are put into action by behaving differently. Even though I am trained as a psychodynamic therapist and Jungian-based analytic art therapist, I have used cognitive behavioral techniques with clients and supervisees for many years. I understand how difficult it is to change individual feelings but how relatively simple it can be to change a detrimental behavior.

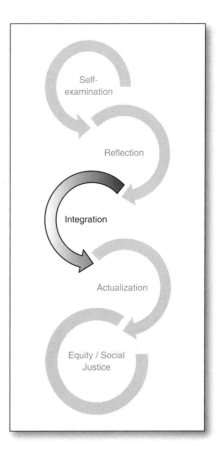

"For most student teachers, in-service teachers, or administrators, the only psychology to which they are generally exposed is exclusively cognitive/behavioral," asserts John Tieman (2007). "We educators tend to think of psychology as a branch of problem-solving. The student does this; you do that. Problem solved." Instead, cognitive restructuring sets about to modify the premises, assumptions, beliefs, and attitudes which underlie a person's thinking and the resulting behaviors that stem from it. In psychotherapy, the purpose of cognitive restructuring is most often focused on those irrational thoughts about one's self. For the purpose of expanding cultural consciousness and equity skill building, cognitive restructuring focuses upon faulty thinking about others. Beck's work focused on cognitive distortions such as unfounded inferences, exaggeration of the significance of an event or situation, disregard or omission of important facts, dichotomous (black/white, good/bad) reasoning, and overgeneralization. Techniques to address cognitive distortions include (1) eliciting and identifying automatic thoughts, (2) testing the validity of automatic thoughts, (3) identifying mistaken and/or maladaptive assumptions, and (4) testing the validity of these assumptions and the veracity of behaviors which result from them. Techniques such as (a) scheduling and repetition, (b) visualization and role playing, (c) thought stoppage, and (d) rehearsal are then used to curtail and ultimately cease or change the dysfunctional behaviors.

Social Perspective Taking (SPT)

Social role-taking, empathic accuracy, everyday mind reading, interpersonal sensitivity—the core construct of SPT entails discerning the thoughts and feelings of others with particular attention to how others perceive the situation. In order for SPT to impact outcomes in the real world, both the ability to read the thoughts and feelings of others accurately and the motivation to engage in SPT frequently are required (Gehlbach, 2010). This is not mind reading (see Guidelines for Clear Communication, page 139), but the ability to read social cueing.

Gehlbach (2010) asserts that *fundamental attribution error, naïve realism,* and *confirmation bias* seem particularly germane to classroom settings. Attribution error refers to the pervasive tendency to explain the social behavior of others by overweighting the causal role of individual personality traits and undervaluing situational causes. Confirmation bias refers to tendencies to seek out and value information that corroborates hypothesis while ignoring or devaluing contradictory information. Naïve realism is the belief that we see objective reality, and those who disagree must be less informed, unwilling to process information fully, or partisan. Mitigating these biases will help educators more accurately perceive their students which, in turn, will enhance pedagogy (Gehlbach, 2010).

Gehlbach (2010) asks how social psychological principles might be realized in teacher education, first noting that these principles need to be adapted into actual classroom practices. Gehlbach writes, "Scholars working within teacher education are uniquely positioned to perform this translation function. They have the background and training in social science research to understand and evaluate social psychological research, and they have a rich understanding of the context in which teachers work," and further asserts that these newly developed classroom practices need to be evaluated. "Because concepts and empirical findings do not always generalize from the laboratory . . . to the classroom, new research needs to assess which applications of social psychological principles transfer" (pp. 358–9).

Giving the example of Piaget, Gehlbach (2010) notes that a conversation about disequilibrium could easily incorporate the broader idea of cognitive dissonance. Piaget's four stages of development—the basis of many child development courses today—involved "cognitive structures," the development of cognition (knowledge) through an individual's process of perpetual organization of information in conjunction with experience. That is, individuals act upon the world and build internal models of the reality based upon these actions and resulting consequences. He perceived systems of mental activity as adaptive knowing which led to the four stages of cognitive development. Intertwined with the notions of assimilation and accommodation (Piaget, 1951), the concepts of equilibrium/disequilibrium/reequilibration also resulted from Piaget's observation that a balance or equilibrium occurs when understanding matches experience. Disequilibrium results when these do not match, causing tension and a need for reequilibration or cognitive restructuring so that understanding and experience are once again in harmony.

Returning to Gehlbach's example, discussions of diversity in classrooms are likely to happen in many teacher education courses naturally, but could also easily lead to a feeling of disequilibrium or cognitive dissonance. Gehlbach (2010) suggests professional development leaders may have more success by suggesting small interventions, showing effectiveness, and building upon those successes in order to implement larger interventions at a later date and writes:

Social interactions lie at the heart of classroom learning. As a result, thoughtful new applications of social psychological principles may have multiple, large, lasting benefits for teachers and students. These applications are needed in schools now more than ever. The current focus on standardized testing and high stakes accountability requires teachers to develop an exceptionally effective, efficient skill set . . . [These principles and applications] provide powerful tools to improve teachers' pedagogy, bolster student motivation, and enrich students' understanding of multiple content areas. Furthermore, depriving teachers of the tools to understand the social dynamics of their classrooms carry a host of costs that schools simply cannot afford. (p. 360)

One of the things that make cognitive restructuring most perplexing is our inability to identify not only *what* our distorted thoughts and feelings are, but *why* we have them in the first place. Basic principles of personal growth can be the best way to begin our transition from cultural carelessness to cultural consciousness and integrate new knowledge and practices. Professional growth calls for personal growth. By beginning to restructure how we feel inwardly, we also restructure how we think and feel outwardly. Diminishing biases about our own abilities gives way to alleviating bias toward others. Self-care is a large portion of this process. In the appendix, we give some basic self-care strategies as guidelines (see page 121).

Learning new frames of reference is difficult enough but when those new frames require the unlearning of old habits of thought, teaching and learning are very "labor intensive" (Kumashiro, 2004, p. 8). Gaven's story shows how laborious and worthwhile cognitive restructuring can be.

Gaven came to see me for anger management issues. He was a well-dressed, polite, and quiet spoken man in his early thirties. He was self-referred rather than court ordered which is typical for men seeking help with their "tempers." After taking some preliminary information, I asked what prompted him to call for the appointment.

He looked down at his hands as if they were separate from him. "I don't know except I'm going to lose my job if I don't get a grip."

I had seen he worked for a local school district but wasn't sure what he did there. "What is your job at the district?"

"I teach eighth-grade history," he answered so softly I could barely hear him.

"What might cause you to lose your grip—and your job?"

A slight smile crossed his face. "You ever teach eighth grade, ma'am?"

"No, I haven't. But I can imagine it might be stressful. You seem like a pretty calm guy, though. What about eighth graders is causing you stress lately?"

"Ah, it's not that bad. I'm not even sure why I called. It's just that I get really angry for no reason. Especially during fifth period. The kids are all starting to get fidgety and this one group of boys start acting like fools. One day last week I got so mad I thought I might punch one of them if the bell hadn't rung." His hands were now clinched and his neck and jaw had tightened.

"What did he say or do to make you so angry?" I asked.

"That's just it. Nothing. They were just boys being boys. The one kid—Nate—wasn't disrespectful or anything. Just something about him. I have this urge to wring his neck."

I asked Gaven to tell me more about his student, Nate. He told me very general things, then described him as "just another kid from the hood."

"What's that mean to you, Gaven?" I was curious as Gaven appeared to be African American.

"I guess I shouldn't say that, should I? But I grew up in the 'hood. He's just like the rest of us used to be; ramblin' through life with no goals, being all cocky and bad ass—sorry, ma'am," he said, catching himself. He had relaxed his speech a little as he became more animated.

"Not to worry," I assured him. "I'm fairly familiar with bad-ass teenagers." He laughed a little, caught off guard by my language. "But I'm wondering if that's why you feel so angry at Nate. It sort of sounds like you expect him to waste his life."

Gaven shook his head and said, "No; I'm sure he's going to waste his life and I don't really care. It's somebody else's life I'm afraid he's going to waste."

"Do you mean waste or kill?"

His expression was one of quiet surprise. "I hope not. But maybe."

"Someone in particular?"

"No. It's just that my brother was in a gang and got involved in some really bad sh— I mean stuff."

"Does Nate remind you of your brother?" I asked. I was concerned about where we might be headed so early, but turning back didn't seem an option either.

"No. It's just that I get to thinking about Gregory and I get so angry I feel like I'm going to explode," Gaven said, his tone measured and deliberate. "Gregory put my mom through hell."

Over the next few sessions, Gaven talked more about his responses to Nate and his friends. He realized that he really knew very little about these students because he either avoided them or reprimanded them, often for "not much reason." Gaven also talked more about his teaching style. He seemed to be a genuinely caring teacher and knowledgeable in his field. In time, he was able to talk about the disappointment he felt in himself that he had no desire to teach these boys and assumed they were uninterested in learning. He was also clear that he wanted to "man up" and "get over it."

Cognitive restructuring worked well for Gaven. He was insightful and could talk about his feelings, but he preferred to solve the problem. He was past thinking that this group of students was the problem and began to work toward changing his own attitudes and behaviors. This began with owning his "faulty thinking" about Nate.

Gaven began to keep a small notebook in his pocket and wrote down every negative thought or feeling he had about Nate. Focusing on one student instead of five was much more attainable and instructive. He brought his notebook to sessions, and we would discuss them. Gaven was *eliciting and identifying automatic thoughts* such as "Nate's a loser" or "Nate's bad news." Thoughts such as "Nate's not interested in learning" were good ones to use for the next step in cognitive restructuring: *testing the validity of automatic thoughts.*

It wasn't easy, but Gaven first began to simply call on Nate in class. At first, Nate was unresponsive but did not act out. Gaven could see that he was actually surprised when his teacher called on him. In a few weeks, Nate started giving some answers to questions. In a few more days, he began to give the right answers. It took about four months for Nate to raise his hand in class to volunteer to lead a group project on the history of the Negro Baseball League.

Gaven was cautiously optimistic. He could *identify mistaken assumptions* about Nate but he wasn't quite ready to trust him. Gaven still found himself angry "for no good reason" at times. Sometimes it was over things like the color of clothing Nate wore or the smell of his hair products. To understand these things better, Gaven began to write short essays. He would then rewrite the essays, reversing his negative feelings and thoughts to positive ones in the story so he could visualize a different outcome. He also began to work out regularly, expending some of the pent-up frustration he recognized was more about his brother, Gregory, than about Nate.

Gaven finally shifted his negative feelings and thoughts about Nate during the class presentation on the Negro League project. Nate was prepared and enthusiastic and led his group well. Gaven even found himself laughing when Nate showed a Photoshopped picture of himself in a St. Louis Stars uniform, and I was delighted when Gaven brought it in to show me.

As Kumashiro (2004) suggested, learning new frames of reference and discarding old habits of thought, teaching, and learning certainly were labor-intensive for Gaven, but his efforts at cognitive restructuring were successful. I suspect they were even more successful for Nate.

Step Five: Expanding Knowledge Base

Expanding knowledge base may be more familiar to educators when it involves hard science, teaching strategies, or pedagogy. To become culturally considerate and conscientious, one must experience different cultures, not just expand one's knowledge of them.

Dr. Christine Sleeter's research focuses on antiracist multicultural education and teacher education. She writes, "Predominantly White institutions have generally responded very slowly to the growing cultural gap." She describes two basic approaches when culture is considered in preservice programs writing, "Preservice programs take two rather different lines of action to address the cultural gap between teachers and children in the school: (a) bring into the teaching profession more teachers who are from culturally diverse communities and (b) try to develop the attitudes and multicultural knowledge base of predominantly White cohorts of preservice students. Although these are not mutually exclusive, they differ in what they emphasize" (C. E., Sleeter, 2001).

Gay (2002) writes, "The knowledge that teachers need to have about cultural diversity goes beyond mere aware of, respect for, and general recognition of the fact that ethnic groups have different values or express similar values in various ways." She discusses the use of "cultural scaffolding" and suggests that teachers need to use students' "own cultures and experiences to expand their intellectual horizons and academic achievement."

Models for teaching diversity content in social work parallel the profession's socio-political history. Pedagogical models in social work programs are perpetually developed and refined to assist students in absorbing diversity content.

Abrams and Gibson (2007) cite Fine (1997) and Sleeter and Bernal (2004) in their observation that teacher education has many parallels with social work education in that both have critics who suggest that a liberal multicultural model has similarly fallen short of exposing future teachers to critical analyses of race and oppression. They also cite Janet Helms' (1990, 1995) theory of racial identity which includes six stages: contact, disintegration, reintegration, pseudoindependence, immersion/emersion, and autonomy.

Racial Identity Development

Janet Helms' oft-cited work—originally in the field of psychology—not only provides instructive models of racial identity development, but also offers a portrait of research in motion. In 1984, Helms introduced her initial models but has continued to elaborate and refine them over the past twenty-five years. Her models differentiate the racial identity development of people of color and the racial identity development of whites based upon what she now calls "statuses." The content of these statuses (formerly termed "stages") is assumed to differ between racial groups due to the power differentials that exist (Helms, 1995).

Using Helms' continuum, racial identities of white social work students and preservice educators may be accomplished in several pedagogical fashions: Teaching About White Identity, Raising Awareness of White Privilege, Building Empathy, and Service Learning (Abrams & Gibson, 2007).

White Privilege

Peggy McIntosh's classic 1988 essay, "White Privilege: Unpacking the Invisible Knapsack," (1989) has been cited extensively and used infinite times in workshops and classes throughout the United States and Canada by those wishing to educate individuals and communities of the vast discrepancy between the experience of white persons and non-white others. McIntosh wrote that white privilege was "an invisible package of unearned assets" about which white people were to "remain oblivious." "White privilege," she wrote, "is like an invisible weightless knapsack of special provisions, maps, passports, codebooks, visas, clothes, tools, and blank checks."

"Many, perhaps most of our white students in the U.S., think that racism doesn't affect them because they are not people of color, they do not see "whiteness" as a racial identity . . . we need similarly the daily experience of having age advantage, or ethnic advantage, or physical ability, or advantage related to nationality, religion, or sexual orientation."

It is hard to disentangle aspects of unearned advantage which rest on social and economic class, race, religion, sex, and ethnic identity than on other factors. White advantage is kept strongly inculturated in the United States so as to maintain the myth of meritocracy—the myth that democratic choice is equally available to all (McIntosh, 1989).

Referencing McIntosh's 1988 article, Solomon, Portelli, Daniel, and Campbell (2005) explored three primary strategies teacher candidates employed to avoid addressing whiteness and its attendant privileges. Believing that "the institutionalization of whiteness and the systemic factors that underscore its continued dominance" socializes whites to conceptualize their world in ways that favor their positions within it, Solomon et al. (2005) identified ideological incongruence, notions of individualism and meritocracy, and the negotiation of white capital as consistent strategies employed in their qualitative study of 200 teacher candidates. This study was designed to help teachers develop the pedagogical insights needed to work for equity, racial diversity, and social justice. A significant issue highlighted for white teacher candidates was that the ideologies that framed their understanding of self and their positioning in society have been socially constructed. The knowledge that their ancestors, using various tools of domination and oppression, have created a society in which their benefits and privileges have been amassed at the expense of other racial and ethnic groups, elicited a sense of confusion and challenged their personal, cultural, and ideological underpinnings which forced them to grapple with seemingly incongruous positions. Another way in which this ideological incongruity was evidenced is the manner in which the sample reframed information to reinforce their ideological bent. This reinforcement was also achieved through a process of discounting information that challenged their belief systems.

Christine Sleeter (2000/2001) views the central issue of white privilege as one of justice. "Multicultural education came out of the civil rights movement . . . the primary issue was one of access to a quality education." She discusses the importance of understanding institutional racism in addition to and apart from psychological explanations of discrimination through examples of tracking systems which ultimately sort students on the basis of both race and social class. "The tracking system is built on presumptions about kids from low-income backgrounds and kids of color; that their parents don't care, they have language deficits, nobody is around to push them with homework. . . . Then we build teaching around that presumption."

Sleeter gives the example of states which have large populations of Hispanic/Latino students. "It's the English reading score that counts, even for kids whose first language is Spanish . . . They're not even thinking in terms of a child's reading ability, but only in terms of their ability to read in English."

Frankenberg (1997) noted that teacher educators often face more resistance when they teach about white privilege than they do when teaching about racism. She stated, "Conscious racialization of others does not necessarily lead to a conscious racialization of the white self . . . whiteness makes itself invisible precisely by asserting its normalcy." In a 1993 study, Frankenberg found three ways of thinking about race: the essentialist racism, color and power evasion (color-blindness), and race cognizance. Essentialist racism sees race as a determinant and explanation of human behavior, color and power evasion recognizes race and status but then dismisses their affects, and finally, race cognizance recognizes the complexities of context, the ways in which race can interact with social-economic status, and the realities of individual identities and experiences.

Abrams and Gibson (2007) advocate the inclusion of white privilege in social work education curriculum, giving an opportunity for interdisciplinary dialog to take place within schools and school communities. They introduce concepts and pedagogical strategies that are, in fact, derived from teacher training programs, asserting that instruction on white privilege is fundamental to understanding systemic oppression and raising self-awareness about social workers' roles and responsibilities with culturally diverse clientele.

Abrams and Gibson (2007) cite the Council on Social Work Education (2005) EPAS 4.2 which stipulates that social work programs must "educate students to identify how group membership influences access to resources" and " . . . provide content related to implementing strategies to combat discrimination, oppression, and economic deprivation and to promote social and economic justice." They recommend the inclusion of content on white identity and privilege across the social work curriculum and argue that teaching about white privilege is fundamental to understanding the oppression and raising self-awareness about practitioners' roles and responsibilities with culturally diverse clientele and communities.

Abrams and Gibson (2007) state that an additional benefit is the opportunity for the majority (white) group of social work students to explore the meaning of their own ethnic and racial identities in relation to those whom they will encounter in their fieldwork and future professional settings.

Intersectionality

Fundamentally, cultural consideration embraces the concept of intersectionality, a term attributed first to legal scholar, Kimberlé Crenshaw. In short, intersectionality is a recognition that no one person has a singular identity. Crenshaw (1989) underscored the "multi-dimensionality of marginalized subjects' lived experiences" (p. 139). Intersectionality emerged from the critical race studies movement, serving theoretic and political purposes for both feminist and antiracist scholarship. By viewing identity in a more complex fashion, intersectionality is attuned to those who "exist . . . within the overlapping margins of race and gender discourse" and captures the simultaneity of race and gender as social processes (Crenshaw, 1992, p. 402). The concept of intersectionality provides a vocabulary which seeks to transcend identity politics and "mediate the tension between assertions of multiple identity and the ongoing necessity of group politics" (Crenshaw, 1991, p. 1296). While intersectionality remains a central theme of feminist scholarship, it has become significant in discussions of intersecting identities of race, ethnicity, class, sexuality, and ability as well.

Intersectionality may be defined as a theory to analyze how social and cultural categories intertwine. The relationship between gender, race, ethnicity, disability, sexuality, class, and nationality are examined. The word *intersection* means that one line cuts through another line as in streets crossing each other (Knudson, 2005).

I introduced my concept of culture in *Culturally Considerate School Counseling: Helping Without Bias,* published by Corwin in 2010. Because of the varied nature of my experiences, I find it difficult to limit my concerns to one issue of equity over another. My experiences—personally and professionally—are the personification of intersectionality. I have come to view and explore culture through

- Heritage and Historic Memory
- Geographic or Regional Origin
- Circumstance and Situation
- Affinity or Relational Bonds

Heritage frames an individual life by providing a familial reference. Historic memory is collective in nature. It is understood as a representation of the past shared by a group or community. Historic memory fosters and defines group identity (Romano, 2009), explaining where members have come from, who they are and how they should behave in the present as it relates to the past.

Romano (2009) further suggests that schools play an important role in shaping collective (historic) memory because they are the first places children learn about important historical events, though most textbooks provide a Eurocentric point of view. For some children and their families, this history is either fictional or biased.

Geographic origin tells us about the place one was born, where one has lived, the terrain traveled. Geography encompasses country, region, state or province, topography, and population distribution. Geographic considerations may skip generations. As with deeply held ancestry, geography can show up in unexpected ways. Customs, idioms, beliefs, and traditions can have strong ties to a family's geographic origins.

Circumstantial considerations include societal structures such as economic status, permanence, and access. Examples include students living in poverty, transient (homeless) families, children in foster care or later-age adoptions, or a student whose parent is incarcerated, indefinitely hospitalized, or otherwise incapacitated.

Affinity or relational bonds may be by choice rather than circumstance, yet there may be an entrenchment in the mores and customs of the group which require consideration. Issues common to most all affinity or relational bonds are a strong sense of allegiance, some measure of uniformity, an actual or implied code of honor, and a suspicion of outsiders—those who are not part of the group or faction (Anderson, 1996 and 2010b).

While "intersectionality" has become a scholarly buzzword, the notion that identity is formed by interlocking and mutually reinforcing vectors of race, gender, class, and sexuality has pervaded black feminist scholarship for decades (Nash, 2008). Nash asserts that it is incumbent upon intersectional scholars to critically interrogate the goals of the intersectional project as they determine how to chart the future of this theoretical and political movement and writes, "The important insights that identity is complex, that subjectivity is messy, and that personhood is inextricably bound up with vectors of power are only an analytic starting point," (Nash, 2008).

Learning Theories and Multiple Intelligences

Most educators, school counselors, social workers and other allied professionals have had basic exposure to theories of human development and learning. Maslow's hierarchy of needs, Piaget's cognitive stages of development, and the later theories of researchers like Bruner, Kolb, and Gardner are the basis of what we know about children and how they take in, perceive, interpret, and communicate information.

Howard Gardner defines intelligence as "the ability to solve a problem or create a product that is valued in a society." In 1983, Gardner proposed an approach to intelligence which suggested there are several different ways to solve a problem. Gardner's theory of multiple intelligences was in sharp contrast to typical, linear theories of intelligence.

In the first chapter of *Frames of Mind: The Theory of Multiple Intelligences* (1983), Gardner, referring to IQ testing of a young girl, states that the outcome "is likely to exert appreciable effect upon her future, influencing the way in which her teachers think of her and determining her eligibility for certain privileges." Our current understanding of diverse learning styles is largely due to Gardner and expanded upon by other scholars. We routinely recognize the specific needs of students whose primary style of taking in information fall into the following categories: linguistic (verbal), musical (auditory), spatial (visual), kinesthetic (bodily or physical), mathematic (logical), interpersonal (social), and intrapersonal (solitary).

In *Frames of Mind,* now in its tenth printing, Gardner delineates types of learning, illustrating how traditional, non-western learning environments emphasis different intelligences from those of European and North American elementary and secondary schools, yet has "elected not to pursue" questions such as whether the intelligences are the same in quality or quantity across groups, i.e., males vs. females or ethnic groups. He defers to the work of others such as Carol Gilligan and Stephen Mithen when it comes to issues of cultural differentiation. How children learn is also important in how they learn to change behavior, understand emotion, and integrate interpersonal skills. This goes for adults as well.

I am excited by David Sousa's (1998) work which includes components of (a) brain growth and development, (b) memory and recall, (c) emotions in learning, (d) sensory engagement, (e) timing, (f) biological rhythms, and (g) learning disabilities. These are components which have been central to my practice with adults and children for over twenty-five years. But I also become concerned when practitioners use "evidence-based best practice" without taking into account the individuality of each student/client. If one child does not respond in a predictable, evidence-based way, we must find a way to reach that student without making him an abnormal variable.

Not unlike my concerns about multicultural training that does not allow for differences within cultural groups of students, I am often confounded by the lack of differentiation when it comes to brain research. In my work, I am privy to the myriad of ways people think and express their thinking. I have never seen two humans who do this in the same way. My task as a clinician and as a staff development consultant is to listen closely to what a person says and find a common means of communicating feelings, thoughts, beliefs, and understandings. This is also our challenge as educators. Yes, there is a body of knowledge that tells us general things about the brain, but even brain researchers admit what we know about the brain is far less than what we don't know.

A simple "fix" from my standpoint is to stop using the singular term "the brain" and use a plural phrase. Perhaps it is because I grew up when Orwell's *1984* was science fiction rather than a decade of bad hair, but I cringe a bit when I hear or read the term "The Brain," as if there is only one in the world and it thinks in anticipated ways and initiates foreseeable behaviors.

Examples of this are found in the current literature which cites the "rapidly changing, multimedia-based culture" which "has a dramatic impact on how the developing brain interprets and interacts with its world" (Sousa, 1998). What, then, does this mean for students who emigrate from countries where electricity is scarce or families where media exposure is limited? What does it mean for a student who has relocated from New Orleans, Louisiana, or Joplin, Missouri, after a devastating natural disaster has destroyed her home while she and her family watched in horror? Do the same brain-based strategies apply?

Bonnie adds . . .

Kim suggests using the plural for brain; what an excellent idea! When we look out over a classroom of students and "brains," we widen our perspective to embrace the differences as the norm. Teaching a classroom of student *brains* might be compared to conducting an orchestra. Even though a teacher works diligently to support the learning of each individual student, she must also balance the engagement and learning of the entire group of students throughout the instructional period. In order to accomplish this, teachers turn to research on pedagogy. One area of instructional pedagogy is commonly referred to in education as brain-based pedagogy. Educators and authors Eric Jensen (2005), David Sousa (2006), and Pat Wolfe (2010), among others, come to mind as experts in this field, and they offer instructional strategies for engaging and "conducting" groups of students through the learning process. When I share brain-based instructional strategies in workshops with teachers, I share such strategies as "wait time," "movement," "choice," and "novelty," among others.

Movement is a favorite of mine since being highly kinesthetic makes it difficult for me to sit and learn from others, and I empathize with students whom teachers require to sit through a 20-minute lecture without time to process both mentally and physically. When teachers use some simple strategies such as asking general questions that require all students to raise their hands or teaching students additional nonverbal hand responses, teachers can embed movement into instruction, allowing students the opportunity to physically move their bodies without disrupting the overall flow of the lesson.

Realizing a teacher is "conducting" an orchestra, rather than giving "private lessons," I asked Kim how teachers can take into account individual needs while accomplishing the task at hand: teaching the content standard to a group of students within a finite period of time. Even though Differentiated Instruction gives teachers multiple ways for students to construct individual learning, there are times when "direct instruction" is necessary, and teachers need to instruct larger groups of students. During these instructional periods, if teachers embed physical movement, they more readily engage the majority of student brains. However, Kim works with students who don't fit the "majority" student group, and she has insights into how teachers might conduct those students within the context of the entire orchestra.

Reflections/Questions

❖ What are some examples of research that supports your instructional practice?
❖ How do you address the need to support each individual learner within the larger classroom group?
❖ What are the strategies that work best for you?
❖ What areas of research might you investigate in the future?

Kim continues . . .

Bonnie refers to my work with students who don't always blend in with the orchestra. The work that has taught me the most about the enormity and expansive capabilities of the human mind is treating adults and children with posttraumatic stress and dissociative identity disorders. As a child therapist, many of my child clients were referred because they very literally danced to the beat of a different drum. In fact, I often use percussion with children in order to identify and stabilize their inner rhythm. The problem, however, is that the way in which a student client finds that rhythm may vary greatly. Many times, they are overstimulated, distracted, or disoriented by the sights and sounds of others.

Bonnie and I have had many discussions about this over time. As an expressive arts psychotherapist and supervisor, I also ascribe value to research and strategies which support theories of multiple intelligences, learning styles, and kinesthetic techniques to enhance personal and professional growth.

Expanding knowledge base not only means learning the hard science of education but also requires expanding our own "soft skills"— another term I would like to see changed. Soft skills (sometimes referred to as *emotional intelligence, critical thinking, interpersonal* or *social skills*) are actually pretty hard. If there is one thing interfering with school environments becoming more culturally conscientious and considerate, it is the hard reality of the absence of these so-called "soft skills."

John Tieman writes of shame in his 2007 article entitled, "The Ghost in the Schoolroom: A Primer in the Lessons of Shame." "Shaming is not a solo. It's a duet. Shaming is done in the context of, in this case, the dyad, the duet, the student and the teacher . . . As we were humiliated, so do we humiliate." Clinically, Tieman is referring to the important and precarious issue of transference and counter-transference within a therapeutic relationship. In the Real World of the classroom, he is describing what happens when our personal baggage flies open and spills onto those around us—especially those who remind us of something or someone representing a negative.

I began my clinical career as an intern in an agency providing services to battered women. I view the issue of bullying very much as I view domestic violence—there cannot be any gray areas when working with batterers. It's not safe for the battered partner. Mediation, couples therapy, and second chances only provide opportunities for the abuser to abuse again and usually—fueled by confrontation, i.e., getting caught—more violently. This also led me to think about the profiles of men (or women) who batter. Very similar to the research on school bullies, they are often personable, popular, and self-confident. If we consider that much of the recent hate speech is coming from the offices of politicians, we might draw the same conclusion. The most integral factor in all circumstances is power.

Power is source dependent. A culturally considerate classroom must create an atmosphere in which all students (and teachers) feel a sense of power and therefore no need to disempower others.

Power rests upon the interpersonal relationship between two persons. Whether a basis of power exists at all and/or how durable it is depends upon how the power holder is viewed by the other.

Drawing upon the classic study by social psychologists John R. P. French and Bertram Raven (1959), sources of power include

- Reward—an ability to gain tangible or intangible favors
- Reference—identification or fondness for the one in power
- Expertise—special knowledge of one above another
- Coercion—threat for noncompliance
- Legitimate—based upon individual (and cultural) values

Signals of power include

- Control Over Space
- Facial Expressions
- Gestures
- Touch
- Who Talks/Who Listens
- Environmental Signals (desks or podiums, keys, signage)
- Economic Control
- Status or Title

Influence exists on a continuum from spontaneous influence because of status to threats which inspire fear. Open influence is just that—open and known to both power holder and recipient. Covert influence is hidden and often insidious, sometimes no better recognized to those in control than those who are manipulated by it. Open influence includes overt promises, predictions, warnings, and threats. Covert influence is subtle and often complex, comprising combinations of manipulation, reinforcement control, and information control in the form of cue control, withholding of knowledge, isolation, and dishonesty.

Often, identification of these methods of influence is viewed and interpreted differently by individuals from different cultures. What is viewed as polite in some cultures may be seen as deceitful in others.

White privilege is both overt and covert influence. White privilege was once overtly the norm as typified by segregated lunch counters and drinking fountains, and violent assaults upon people of color. Today, white privilege can be clearly seen in hate speech, offhanded slurs by entertainers, anti-Muslim demonstrations. Sometimes it is more subtle, such as questioning a president's birthplace or a Supreme Court justice's Latina wisdom.

Each day, educators and counselors exert influence over children. In truth, this is the nature of the job. But when a child or adolescent is influenced directly or indirectly to feel he or she is less than because of skin color, religion, ability, emerging sexuality, or socioeconomic circumstances, the lessons are damaging and far reaching. Born out of ignorance and fear, oppression thrives on oppression. Singleton and Linton (2006) write, "As White educators normalize multiple points of view, they come to a much deeper understanding of the cumulative effect of racism for people of color." Singleton and Linton also point out that typically, "White educators fill the room with ideas for improving the achievement of students of color, but their ideas often are not welcomed or supported by their colleagues of color." They note that, "As an American culture, we often recognize, embrace, and promote people of color whose racial ideology is aligned with more conservative White ideologies" (p. 109).

Cultural Considerations for Integration

- Invite each student to create an illustrated dictionary of important words in their personal vocabulary and include slang or colloquial terms. Asking students to share their innate knowledge allows them to be experts. Admitting that we are not knowledgeable in some areas gives a child or adolescent an opportunity to experience a level playing field. When a teacher asks to be taught, he or she models how to ask questions or for help in culturally sensitive manners.

- Write a sentence using each of the slang words then ask your students to "grade" your work. Making ourselves vulnerable in front of children and adolescents takes courage. Taking the risk of being wrong or silly can be quite appealing to students. It also allows them more freedom to be wrong or silly.

- Invite students to make a list of the spices in their kitchen. Identify one or two with which you are unfamiliar and ask each student to bring in a teaspoon of that spice and a family/household recipe which includes it. Food is a universal bonding agent. By sharing the things that make a meal, a "meal of imagination" is created (Anderson, 1998/2007).

- Create an Oral History Night and invite parents and grandparents in to tell about their experience of historical events. Giving authority to each student's individual family and showing respect to elders elevates the elder but also the child by association. Giving voice to a collective history not only provides a forum for collective memory from which students can gather knowledge about their own heritage but also that of their peers.

- Invite local authors or entertainers from various neighbor-hoods and cultural backgrounds to come into the class-room and interact with students. Similar to Oral History Night, this activity gives voice and theater to a collective culture. Children and adolescents can often retain informa-tion when it has entertainment as well as intellectual value. Venues in which they can participate through sing-along or active roles are particularly productive.
- Ask your students to identify the needs of their communi-ties. Identify a common theme and create a service learning project that will touch as many diverse communities as possible. Sharing common struggles supports the develop-ment of empathic understanding. Discovering common solutions supports critical thinking and problem-solving skills, both essential to conflict resolution.

7

Actualization

Step Six: Skill Building

Skill building actualizes culturally considerate education by implementing strategies found within texts or workshops. By providing concrete steps teachers can and must take to infuse their pedagogy with equity, this chapter urges readers to (a) challenge the status quo of their school culture, (b) become an identified advocate of cultural consideration, and (c) lead the discussion of multiculturalism and diversity whether one on one or in faculty meetings. Bonnie includes relationship strategies, content-specific instructional strategies, and research-based instructional strategies in a format palatable to classroom teachers and building administrators. We understand a bridge must be constructed from research to knowledge to practical classroom application in order for change to occur. An educator may think he

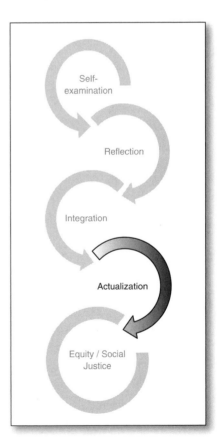

"knows and understands equity" but unless he can demonstrate this within the classroom with students, equity remains abstract and does not impact student achievement nor does it contribute to an equitable school community.

So much of what we bring into the classroom, the school counseling office, or faculty meetings is from our own experience of being a child or a teenager within an academic setting. We try to think we are *beyond it . . . in control . . . it doesn't matter . . . older and wiser,* but such thoughts only get in the way of mastering our internal classroom. In order to bring ordered and productive learning into the external classroom, we have to make peace with our internal one.

As we have seen on pages 30–35, our personal/professional cultural biographies reflect the intersectionality of our history and historic memory, geography and regional origin, circumstances and situation, and affinity and relational bonds for our students. We must recognize the impact of these influences in our own development. Many books and workshops ask that we explore our racial identity and assert it to be an important portion of our development but this is the beginning of cultural consideration, not the totality of it.

Cultural Self-Awareness Matrix

History & Historic Memory   Geography & Regional Origins

Circumstances & Situation   Affinity & Relational Bonds

Figure 7.1   Cultural Self-Awareness Matrix

Before considering the cultures of our students, we must consider our own. In my workshops, I use the Cultural Self-Awareness Matrix (Anderson 2010a) which I designed to help participants clarify their own cultural identity before we begin to address the identities of others. A blank copy of this matrix may be found on page 135.

Bonnie is extremely aware of her white female privilege. I am not so aware of mine, even though I, too, am white and female. As we discussed this, Bonnie thought perhaps this was due to my non-normative aesthetics—beauty in our dominant culture is extraordinarily important. This is a factor, of course, but what is more significant in my cultural matrix is the historic memory of the Great Depression and my maternal lineage of poverty as a result.

My mother was born in the mid-1930s, and her family struggled. When my grandparents divorced in the early 1940s, it was not only considered a rare occurrence with attached stigma, but it created an extreme financial hardship on my grandmother and her children.

My grandmother was a quiet, proud woman. She refused help from others and took it only when her children were hungry. She missed many a meal so that my mother and her siblings would not.

While this impoverished, single-parent existence was a great source of embarrassment for my grandmother, my mother, and her siblings, I took away a sort of idealization of poverty. In addition, my great-grandmother had been widowed for many years, necessitating the need to work and support herself in the 1940s and '50s. These were my heroines, making the most of the meager and doing it on their own without men. What I didn't understand until much later was the guilt, shame, and grief these life circumstances brought them. Today, I understand the dignity of people in poverty juxtaposed to inaccessibility because of it.

In addition to cultural self-awareness, awareness of our individual experiences of school can help to clarify the internal classroom we carry with us. Simple things like favorite teachers, hardest subjects, the view from your seat, or lunchroom odors can be very informative. For example, I both loved and hated second grade. I loved the fact that my best friend and I were ahead of my class in every subject because we had transferred from other schools with more advanced curricula. I also hated it because I spent the entire semester without skin on my knees because the school had a concrete playground and I fell down *a lot*. While the academic reinforcement was great for my intellectual self-esteem, the wounds to my athletic prowess were significant and I was timid in PE classes for many years.

To begin to discover your internal (internalized) classroom, consider these questions:

- What grade did you enjoy most?
- What grade did you enjoy least?
- Where did you sit in the classroom and why?
- What kind of student were you?
- What did you bring to school with you each day?
- What did you have in your lunch box?

By considering these questions, we can begin to visualize the classroom we carry with us inside each day. Understanding how our internal classrooms contribute to the external classroom we create can help us to avoid problems before they arise or to capitalize on those aspects which can enhance both.

So much of what we convey is done non-verbally, though even when we use words we don't always have an emotional vocabulary.

Wholistic Reflection Worksheet

I think _____
_____

(What my mind tells me about this person, event, situation, or problem.)

I feel _____
_____

(The emotions I feel and the physical sensations I have in my body in response to this situation.)

I know _____
_____

(Considering my thoughts and feelings, what facts have I concluded.)

I believe _____
_____

(What does my intuition or faith tell me in regard to this person, event, situation, or problem.)

Figure 7.2 Wholistic Reflection Worksheet

Cultural Consideration Event Summary Date _____

Description of Event
_____
_____
_____
_____
_____
My First Thoughts _____
My Body Felt _____
I Knew _____
I Believed _____
What I Wanted to Do _____
What I Did _____
Result _____
What I Will Do Next Time
_____
_____

How I Feel About How I Handled Things
_____
_____
_____

Figure 7.3 Cultural Consideration Event Summary

Emotions generally can be described by five simple words: happy, sad, angry, fearful, and confused. Beyond that, other words give clarity and nuance. Expanding our own emotional vocabulary helps to clarify why we feel what we feel and differentiate the extent to which we feel it. When we as teachers and helpers use a broader vocabulary, we teach by example and model the effectiveness of communicating more clearly.

On page 136 we have provided a list of feeling words along with a list of body signals which can be helpful when beginning to expand our emotional vocabulary. After becoming comfortable with these lists, try to add at least one new word each day to expand your vocabulary even further.

Sometimes our bodies know what we feel before our brains translate it into words. Learning how our body communicates is important in deciphering what we feel. Paying attention to when our bodies feel tired, tense, achy, or anxious can be the first hint of emotional conflict. Do you find your jaw tightening or teeth clinching when certain students approach your desk? Do you become jittery during consultation with a colleague whose beliefs are different than yours? When your male principal stops by to audit your classroom performance, do you feel dizzy or nauseous?

These body signals can tell us when we have strong reactions to a person or a situation. Becoming more aware of when these responses occur and attaching specific words to them can help us to identify potential problems and address them before they get out of hand. I use very basic worksheets with child clients as well as adult supervisees when we are trying to figure out why they are having difficulty: the Thoughts and Feelings Reflection Worksheet and Event Summary. I have adapted them here for use in conflicts of cultural consideration. The Event Summary includes the date and the time of day because we each have individual biorhythms which are important to how we feel and interact. It also includes simple reflections: what was happening; emotions about what was happening; how my body was feeling; what I thought about doing; what I did (or didn't do); and how I feel about the outcome. A sample of the log can be found on page 132 of the appendix.

Also found in the appendix is a list of Feelings and Body Signals. These are modest lists of words to jump-start our emotional and kinesthetic vocabularies. Another tool I use with clients and in almost every training workshop is a Wholistic Reflection Journal which is loosely adapted from Carl Jung's Four Functions (1921/1971). Often in response to evocative questions or art making, I will invite participants to spontaneously finish the following sentences: I think . . . , My body feels . . . , I understand . . . , and I believe. . . . These statements can reveal four distinct aspects of ourselves—mind, body, psyche, spirit—which merge to reflect how we *consider* a person, situation, or the world around us. A sample of these journal sheets can be found on page 133.

To Cordova and Matthiesen (2010), it seems harder than ever for teachers and students to create learning communities that honor students' and teachers' lived experiences as funds of knowledge to build upon as readers and writers and researchers. They examined ways in which an innovative professional learning community provided important consequences for professionals and for students. They also present how these efforts support diverse teachers from diverse settings, across urban and rural settings, serving as resources for one another in meeting the challenges presented by a common "narrowing of curriculum" and pedagogical options.

Cordova & Matthiesen (2010) cite Crocco and Costigan (2007) who argued that what has been called "the narrowing of what counts as curriculum [the impact of mandated and prescribed curriculum that frequently limits pedagogical options]" has meant that new teachers in many urban schools "often find their personal and professional identity development thwarted, creativity and autonomy undermined, and ability to forge relationships with students diminished." They further argued that this, in turn, may have real consequences for teacher retention in these urban settings. Cordova and Matthiesen (2010) assert this narrowing of curriculum and of pedagogical options, therefore, has potential serious consequences for what comes to count as the teaching and availability of opportunities for learning literacies in urban classroom settings.

Bonnie writes about Culturally Considerate Teaching

How can teachers become fluent in the literacies needed to teach in urban settings, or any setting for that matter? Finding teacher models who practice Culturally Considerate teaching and using them as guides is one way to build our repertoire of skills.

How is Culturally Considerate teaching actualized in the classroom? I had the opportunity to learn firsthand not long ago when I met and then observed a culturally considerate teacher.

I am often struck by the simplicity of the comments of good teachers. One such man, upon meeting me in a workshop, told me how much he liked the students and enjoyed teaching them. I was a bit surprised which told me I had expectations he would begin the conversation by complaining about these high school students since it was near the end of the school year and he taught in a challenging high school of diverse students. He said he had been teaching only four years, and so I asked him what it was he enjoyed about teaching and his students. His answer was so simple and elegant, yet it spoke to a person who was practicing culturally considerate engagement with students. These were his reasons: he said being older gave him an advantage because of his life experience; he said he taught computer courses and all his work was project-based; he said he tells the students at the beginning of the semester that his students make As because everyone finishes every project because he works with them until they complete the projects, even if it means working before school, during lunch, or after school; he said he tells them the only way they cannot make good grades in his classes is to not come to class. I asked him why he came to the Saturday workshop on a beautiful May day. He said he wants to learn all he can about teaching.

This teacher articulated culturally considerate teaching by doing the following:

❖ Meeting the students where they are and knowing they come to his class with different cultures, abilities, and degrees of motivation
❖ Providing each individual student with the scaffolding to achieve success with each assigned project
❖ Working with students one-on-one outside of class time to achieve results—this shows the students he truly cares about them
❖ Offering a classroom environment to students where they experience success—nothing motivates like success

I admired him for his openness to learn and change. He is a lifelong learner and mirrors the definition of a culturally considerate classroom teacher.

He also provided me with an opportunity to check out my own preconceptions and prejudices. I truly expected the teachers in this workshop to come in complaining. His conversation with me caused me to realize I stereotyped the staff (and the students!) at this high school rather than approaching each staff member and student as an individual and truly listening to them and interacting with them as individuals.

Questions

❖ What about this teacher says to you that he actualizes cultural consideration in his work?

❖ What things do you do to actualize culturally considerate interactions with your students?

❖ What things do you do to actualize culturally considerate instruction within your lessons?

❖ What is one new thing you might try to further actualize culturally considerate pedagogy?

Culturally Considerate Teaching: Algebra Class

The following example focuses on concrete strategies the teacher uses to engage her students, teach the lesson, check for understanding, give feedback, and culturally respect her class.

The teacher greets each student warmly at the door, using the students' names and pronouncing them clearly and correctly. She doesn't shorten James to Jim or Andrew to Andy unless the student asks her to call him by the shortened name. After the students have found their seats, she begins class with a ritual to build community and focus the students' brains on the work at hand. She checks in with each student by asking a general question of the class related to the lesson book and brings all students on board: every student gets an opportunity to respond in class and each voice is heard and valued; there are no wrong answers; the teacher learns new information about the students; the students practice good listening skills; the students learn more about each other; and the activity builds on the classroom community. Since they are reviewing fractions, she asks: "Give an example of a fraction of something you interacted with during the past 24 hours." Students answered things such as one eighth of a pizza; one half of a locker; one twentieth of a book; one fiftieth of a toothpaste tube, etc.

The teacher then uses a nonverbal command to transition to the next activity. She begins her mini-lesson with questions for the students to pique their interest, build background knowledge, and motivate each student to raise his/her hand at some point to answer. She then tells the students *What* they are going to learn and asks them to repeat back to her *What* they are going to learn: by doing this, she "frames the lesson." They repeat back to her *What* they are going to learn, and she adds *Why* they are going to learn the new concept. She asks them to repeat to each other *Why* they are going to learn the new concept. She then asks them to relate the *What* and the *Why* to their own lives: Why should they be interested in learning the new information? After students connect the learning to their own lives, she asks for two or three students to share their connections with the entire class. Both the "check-in" and the "framing of the work" take less than five minutes. Students are now visible and part of the larger learning community; they have stated a "right" answer out loud in front of their peers; and they know what and why they are learning today. No student is left invisible; no student has his/her head down at the back of class.

She then begins the lesson. She uses the names of the students throughout her direct instruction.

The teacher continues to teach the new concept and continually checks for understanding. In this case, she is using "white boards" for the students to write their answers on. Each student has a white board; each student does the problem on the white board and then holds it up for the teacher to check. The teacher walks around the room and gives immediate, concrete, specific feedback to the students. If a student's answer is incorrect, he has time to rewrite his answer and hold up the new response.

The teacher keeps the pace brisk in class, moving throughout the room, checking answers. After all students' answers are checked and are correct, the teacher moves on. The students are 100% engaged because their hands are busy writing on the white boards and holding them up for the teacher to check. During the class, the teacher has incorporated physical movement by using the white boards. She also demonstrated proximity by walking about the room to check the students' answers.

After the practice period, the teacher assigns more complex problems to student groups, and students work together to find the correct answer. But before they begin, the teacher shares how she doesn't always do every math problem successfully, and that is why working in a group supports our learning. She stresses collaboration rather than competition. She tells the students they are all responsible for each member of the class. Only when everyone succeeds will they be a successful class.

The students appreciate her candor and begin their work together. Each group has a leader who goes to the board and shares the group problem on the board. The teacher has divided the board into eight areas with colored masking tape so as to give each group a clear space for recording the problem. The students are engaged because they are all involved in solving the problems, and now their team leader is up in front of the class showing their work. Each student feels involved, visible, successful.

The teacher concludes the lesson by connecting the learning to their lives. How can they use what they learned today in their neighborhoods and communities? The students discuss the connections to their real world lives.

The teacher assigns the homework, then tells the students their excellent work ethic caused them to finish a bit early so they have five minutes to share. The teacher begins the sharing in a format she calls, "For the Good of the Group." For the Good of the Group is a strategy where any student is allowed to express an opinion. One student talks at a time, and the comments must be appropriate and not include any negative comments about individuals. The teacher models For the Good of the Group by telling her class (and remember, she is a math teacher) how much she enjoyed reading *Hunger Games,* and she suggests they read it. She piques their interest with a 30-second book talk about *Hunger Games* and invites responses. Students follow with their responses.

The teacher cues the students that the bell is to ring. She tells them to complete their exit slips which they write on Post-it Notes. The students were asked to write (1) what did you learn today? (2) what were you supposed to learn? and (3) what do you need help on?

They gather their materials. She goes to the door and stands there to collect the exit slips. As each student hands her an exit slip, she says the student's name and gives a positive comment, such as, "You were really working hard today, Michael."

The students leave with smiles on their faces. They leave a class where they were visible to the teacher; they were actively engaged in the learning; they experienced success; they worked in groups with peers; and they had a voice in the room at the beginning of class, during class, and at the end of class. The teacher received feedback from the answers on the students' white boards; the problems recorded on the boards by the student groups; and the remarks on the exit slips.

What strategies might you try with your students? Consider choosing one strategy to implement within the next week. Observe the outcomes from using the strategy. Share with colleagues.

Cultural Considerations for Actualization

- Consider additional steps to gain mastery over your internal classroom. Make a seating chart of your current classroom. On a scale of 1 to 3 (1 = Comfortable, 2 = Neutral, 3 = Uncomfortable), designate your cultural comfort with each student by placing the number by his or her name. Visualization is a powerful tool in "seeing" the internal results of our biases. To borrow from an addiction model— because it is easy to become reliant upon "stinkin' thinkin'— taking a rigorous inventory of our limitations, attitudes, and behaviors toward others is a powerful step toward consideration of others and healing cultural wounds. While this is not a strategy to be shared with students, it is one which can greatly benefit them. By awareness of our level of discomfort with any given student or student group, we can begin to explore and shift our unconscious thoughts and attitudes. Looking at our biases head-on reduces denial, expands awareness, and opens possibilities for growth.

- Establish a classroom of respect. Discuss with your students the *why* of respect: why you must respect yourself, each other, the teacher, and the act of teaching and learning. As with any other lesson, students retain information more effectively with repetition, understanding of how and why something works, and how to integrate it into everyday life.

- Declare your space a Culturally Considerate Classroom. Let your students and colleagues know that name calling, derogatory comments, or intrusive behavior are not welcome. Post pro-active, positive messages throughout the classroom via signs, posters, and art work. Pictures not only are worth a thousand words, but in this day of visual inundation, they are essential to communicate clearly and directly with children *and* adults.

- Share incidents of concern with your students. Take caution not to "shame the shamer," but don't hold back naming cultural insensitivity when you see or hear it. Explain how you felt when it happened and what you thought. Ask the student who initiated the insensitive act to describe his or her feelings at the time. Try your best to have empathy for those feelings as well as the student who was the brunt of the act. This models accepting others for where they are, even if it is unfamiliar or offensive to us.

8

Equity & Social Justice

Step Seven: Culturally Considerate Practice

Culturally considerate practice (education without bias) requires manifestation of what has been learned. Cultural consideration is useless without demonstrative action. Students, families, colleagues, administration, and community must be able to identify educator capabilities as professionals who are open to all students and strive to teach without bias. To truly be competent, one must acknowledge there is always more to learn. Bonnie writes, "Knowing what I don't know I don't know continues to expand rather than diminish my life" (Davis, 2006).

In order for school to be a safe and nurturing place for both students and teachers, establishing parameters of a safe and unbiased learning environment can make all the difference. Not only does it set the tone and

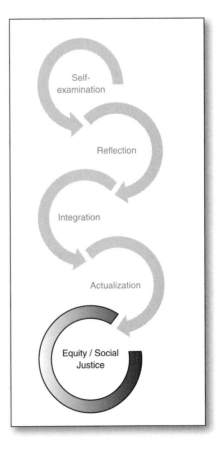

pace of a classroom or of a single lesson, but it allows everyone to start from the same place of peaceful entry. We made reference to our rules of engagement earlier in the book and we have adapted them for the classroom as follows:

Arrive Unencumbered. Do your best to leave concerns of home at the door. Remember that you are essentially entering special space and as guardians of that space, you have a duty to yourself and your students to focus upon them and the lessons of the day.

Enter With Intent. Consider what you would like to impart to your students and what you would like to receive from the experience. This may shift and change, but keep your original focus in mind. Often our first instinct is our best.

Self-Care. If you have special needs, make sure you attend to them, being considerate of others in the process. If others have special needs, be considerate but don't sacrifice your own comfort. Consideration does not mean martyrdom.

Respect Others. Be respectful of differing opinions, communication styles, and distinct voices.

Circulate. Get to know your colleagues and your students beyond the subject they teach or the placement of their desk.

Ask Questions. If you don't understand something model appropriate and *considerate* inquiry by asking for explanation or elaboration.

Leave Satisfied. Just as you arrived unencumbered, do your best to leave school at school. Don't take things home with you or to the next class. They will be there tomorrow. This will not only make your evening more pleasant but you will find that the next day, or next hour, will be better as well. Some teachers find this impossible to consider, but others manage to do it.

These rules of engagement can also be found in the Appendix beginning on page 138, along with several other resources that one or both of us use on a regular basis. They are in formats easily shared with others, posted on bulletin boards, or on blogs and list serves. A few are summarized in the following pages.

Personal Rights

We all have the basic right to be treated with respect, the right to say "no," and the right to make mistakes. These are human rights, not privileges. We also have the right to clear communication which includes: respect of one another, honesty, equal time, "I" statements, clarification, admitting and accepting mistakes.

Personal Rights

The Right to Promote One's Own Dignity and Self Respect
The Right to be Treated with Respect by Others
The Right to Say "No"
The Right to Experience and Express One's Feelings
The Right to Take Time to Think before Acting
The Right to Change One's Mind
The Right to Ask for What One Wants
The Right to Achieve Less than is Humanly Possible
The Right to Ask for Information
The Right to Make Mistakes
The Right to Feel Good About One's Self

Figure 8.1   Personal Rights

Guidelines for Clear Communication

Clear communication does *not* include name calling, generalizations, "you" statements, threats or intimidation, assumptions, or expecting a winner or loser. Communication often is derailed by habit, fear of displeasing someone, guilt and/or shame, misinformation about personal rights, abuse, violence or secrets. Causes of poor communication can be anger, misinformation/ignorance, lack of empathy for the other person, mistrust and enjoyment of control. Cultural differences also can result in communication deficits. Geneva Gay (2002) writes that "determining what ethnically diverse students know and can do, as well as what they are capable of knowing and doing, is often a function of how well teachers can communicate with them."

Additional considerations for communication have to do with body language, affect, and special boundaries such as facial expressions, gestures, touch, tone and volume of voice. Consider these communication guidelines when approaching your students, their parents, colleagues, and administration. Pay specific attention to cultural differences in space, voice volume, eye contact, and means of addressing one another.

Cordova & Matthiesen (2010) write,

Research focused on the mismatches and clashes in cultural expectations between home and school sheds light on how to

Guidelines for Clear Communication

Clear communication includes
- Respect of one another
- Being honest
- Speaking one at a time and allowing equal time
- "I" statements
- Clarifying by repeating
- Giving reasons
- Making compromises
- Admitting mistakes
- Time-outs and taking breaks
- Observing the guidelines agreed upon

Clear communication does *not* include
- Name calling
- Generalizations
- "You" statements
- Tangents
- Violence, threats, or intimidation
- Changing the rules
- Expecting a winner and loser
- Expecting a right or wrong
- Saving up issues and dumping them all at once
- Mind reading
- Assumptions
- Denying the facts
- Gloating over a victory
- Stonewalling or ignoring the other person

Barriers to communication include
- Habit
- Fear of displeasing someone
- Mistaken sense of responsibility
- Protecting the other person
- Guilt and/or shame
- Misinformation about personal rights
- Reluctance to give up benefits of silence
- Financial insecurity
- Chemical abuse or dependency
- Abuse or violence
- Secrets

Causes of poor communication are
- Anger
- Depression
- Misinformation/ignorance
- Feelings of vulnerability
- Lack of empathy for the other person
- Mistrust of the other person
- Control feels good

Additional communication considerations:
- Facial Expressions
- Gestures
- Touch
- Interrupting
- Tone and volume of voice
- Control over space

Figure 8.2   Guidelines for Clear Communication

understand and work with frame clashes that teachers may experience in their everyday work with youngsters with backgrounds different from their own. Teachers may be aware of these differences, yet they often struggle to transform their learning from this level of knowing to the level of informed professional action. Thus, as literacy educators, how teachers conceptualize texts matter and whose texts they choose to value matters even more . . . When teachers do this . . . they are guiding students to navigate the cultural expectations and demands embedded within the official curriculum, but honoring their own lived experiences as resources for academic learning . . . [and] create new spaces [that] allow the in-school official script to be expanded and made accessible to students, who bring to it a sense that they too have rich experiences. (p. 456)

Similar to Gay's culturally responsive teacher preparation program components, achieving culturally considerate practice includes "knowledge about the linguistic structure of various ethnic communication styles as well as contextual factors, cultural nuances, discourse features, logic and rhythm, delivery, vocabulary usage, role relationships of speakers and listeners, intonation, gestures and body movements," (Gay, 2002). In addition to utilizing the resources provided here, we suggest revisiting the section on sources of power and influence as outlined on page 71.

Conflict Resolution and Problem Solving

Conflict Resolution

- Deal with one issue at a time.
- Set a time limit.
- Follow the guidelines for clear communication and rigidly abide by them.
- Stay current. Do not talk about past problems unless they directly relate to the present.
- Allow both talking and listening time.
- Do not interrupt.
- Arrive at a solution good for both parties. A problem has not been solved if someone has to "give in" for the sake of ending a conflict.

Figure 8.3 Conflict Resolution Guidelines

Using standardized guides for conflict resolution and problem solving can be helpful in moving a difficult conversation along to a helpful conclusion. Dealing with one issue at a time, setting time limits, allowing equal time, and staying on topic are all essential to a fair and productive conversation. A problem has not been solved if someone has to "give in" for the sake of ending a conflict. Yet we also acknowledge that even these guidelines may need to adapt to cultural variables. One such example may be seen within the issue of staying current. When a person of majority culture "stays current" it may be interpreted through the lens of what researchers call

"topic-centered" communication, a predomi-
nately linear, logical, Eurocentric male style of
address. Many African, Asian, Latino, and
Native Americans use a different approach to
organizing and transmitting ideas sometimes
referred to as "topic-chaining." This style
of communication is contextual, uses background information, symbolism and metaphor,
and embeds talk with feelings of intensity and
aesthetics (Gay, 2002).

Problem Solving Steps

1. Define the problem.
2. Specify the desired outcome.
3. List ways to attain the goal.
4. Narrow the focus to the top three choices.
5. List positives and negatives of each choice.
6. Calculate findings.
7. If things remain unclear, re-examine the problem definition and desired outcomes. It may be that the core issue[s] have not been stated clearly.

Figure 8.4   Problem Solving Steps

Bonnie adds . . .

Teachers want to know what culturally relevant instruction looks like and sounds like.
They hear the phrase "culturally relevant" yet do not understand what that means.
In a workshop I did in a high-achieving school district that had been working with
equity issues for eight years, the number one question from the teachers in the workshop was, "What makes a strategy 'culturally relevant?'" Kim and I broaden the definition of the culturally relevant strategy to include what makes a research-based
strategy "culturally considerate"? We believe a research-based culturally considerate
strategy is one which has been proven to be research-based (it works to raise student
achievement) while it honors individual and cultural differences.

Culturally Considerate Classroom Practices

❖ Allow for every voice in the room to be heard both aurally and in written form
❖ Set up the lesson to reduce stress and threat so all students function on a more level
  playing field
❖ Engage the cultures of the students in learning activities reinforced by their cultures
❖ Seek to teach the content through the modalities reinforced by their cultures
❖ Allow students to interact with other students during the lessons
❖ Include representative role models from students' cultures
❖ Seek to eliminate language that reinforces one culture over another
❖ Offer choice in order for each student to work to the best of his or her abilities
❖ Use consistent protocols in order for each student to work to the best of his or her abilities
❖ Incorporate a relationship-building piece to the lesson in order to connect to all
  students
❖ Utilize proximity and movement during the lesson
❖ Post visuals of role models from the content discipline of diverse cultures
❖ Demonstrate respect that translates to the diverse cultures of the students
❖ How might this actually *look?*

Culturally Considerate Teaching in a Content Area

Because I taught English for thirty years, these personal examples come from classes focused on reading and writing. However, consider brainstorming with colleagues to create lessons in other disciplines which honor students' brains, cultures, and selves.

A Culturally Considerate Introduction to a Poetry Unit

When I taught poetry in middle and high school classes, I began the unit by bringing in as many poetry books as I could find from my own library, the school's library, the public library, and other teachers' libraries. I usually had over 100 books in the room, and I piled them into a large group in the center of the room. When students entered, they saw piles of books and lots of new posters on the walls—posters of poets from diverse cultures, demographics, genders, etc. They spent the first day of the poetry unit picking up books and looking through them—touching them, feeling them, reading snippets of poems, showing lines to others, laughing, quietly digesting lines, connecting with poetry. By the end of the class period, each student chose a poem he or she enjoyed to share with others. This allowed the students lots of choice; time to share with their peers; a relaxed atmosphere which lowered stress and threat; and the opportunity to be introduced to the wonderful world of poetry through their own construction of meaning.

I sat down with the students and spent the time as they did looking through and enjoying reading poems from a variety of books. After about twenty minutes, we began to share. I modeled a favorite poem and then took volunteers from the students. Most students shared on the first day, and by the time they left the class, students had heard twenty poems or so from the mouths of their peers and recommended by their peers. What better way to have them want to learn more about poetry?

Additional Culturally Considerate Ideas for the Poetry Unit:

- ❖ Ensure that all the cultures of the students were represented in the books of poetry available to the class.
- ❖ Include a variety of poetry books in the languages of the students as well as bilingual books of poetry.
- ❖ Introduce some poets from the cultures of the students.
- ❖ Post visuals of the culturally diverse poets.
- ❖ Ask for volunteers to read poetry in other languages.
- ❖ Do a mini-lesson on the Poets who have won the Nobel Prize, who are Nobel Laureates, etc., so that students are aware that poets come in all colors, ethnicities, and genders.

Of course, things have changed in the past decade, and students now can use their smartphones, computers, and other media to do what we did with paperback books. Rather than begin with a pile of poetry books, you may begin by asking students to search the web for their favorite poems. They can bookmark websites and compile lists of their favorites to share during class similarly as they would have shared poems from a book.

Culturally Considerate Writing Instruction

In teaching writing, I searched for numerous ways to make the lessons culturally considerate. In *How to Teach Students Who Don't Look Like You: Culturally Relevant Teaching Strategies* (Davis, 2006), I list several lessons in literacy that include culturally considerate instruction. Fortunately, with the teaching of writing, one can always use the student as the resource for the subject. Following are some suggestions:

❖ Have students write themselves into the book they're reading. Suggest they find a compelling section of the book, a part that speaks to them, and add themselves to the list of characters. They only need to describe their part in the action, the plot, and incorporate it into the actual text. They can keyboard three pages from the text and then add their part in sections where it best fits the plot. They love doing this because they now become one of the farmhands in *Of Mice and Men,* one of the kids on the island in *The Lord of the Flies,* another kid on the block in *The House on Mango Street,* etc. Once they write themselves into the story, it gains interest for them and creates student buy-in and engagement.

❖ Ask students to write personal journals. Student journals give students a place to record their thoughts, describe their culture, and relate their hopes and dreams (goals). They can share the journals with the teacher, peers, or just themselves. The journal becomes a treasure chest of story ideas for creative pieces.

❖ Assign an oral history based on an adult in the student's community. This offers students the opportunity to learn about their community, the elders in their community, and the hopes and dreams of the community.

❖ Create a Guidebook to the lesson. Have students create their own guidebooks for what they need to learn. Have them illustrate them, add vocabulary, embed learning strategies, etc. When students reflect on how they learn and create a guide for their learning, they increase their student engagement.

❖ Round-robin story writing. Have students begin a story and pass it on. Each student adds a paragraph. You may want to put the students on teams of the number of paragraphs you want in the story. The students write, pass it on, and then share with others. This is a fun way to fill some time and keep students working and engaged.

❖ Buffet Table: On Fridays, ask students to place what they wrote during the week on a "buffet" table where students can select what they want to read. Students put their stories (without their names) on the table. Students spend most of the class period reading the writings of others. At the end of each writing, students add a sentence which states what they "liked" about the anonymous student's writing. At the end of the class, students retrieve their papers and have an enjoyable time reading the positive comments from their peers.

Culturally Considerate Classroom Reading

To create a classroom where students relate culturally to the reading, the teacher need only to employ a variety of strategies to connect students to the reading material and methods for reading it. If the teacher ensures her library of books in the classroom reflects the cultures of her students, that is a beginning. Just imagine you must learn each day in a classroom with only books written in Boatatolese and about Boatatola. Unless you are from Boatatola or know Boatatolese, you will feel disconnected, yet we expect students whose first language is not English and who may not be from the United States to adapt quickly to our classrooms. What if, instead, the classroom library reflected the cultures of all the students in the room, had phrases from all of their languages posted around the room, and had pictures of each student posted somewhere on the walls? That classroom would welcome students.

To create a classroom that prizes reading, the teacher needs to read to the students. Students can also read to the class in their native languages, and rather than an opportunity for shame, the students can be proud to be bilingual and bicultural. When students are made to feel pride in their home language and country, they are more apt to engage in the instruction in the classroom.

Questions

- ❖ What are some culturally responsive strategies that work for you?
- ❖ Describe how you might take a current successful strategy and tweak it to make it more culturally considerate.
- ❖ How do you ensure the cultural visibility of each of your students each and every day in the classroom?
- ❖ How do you level the social justice and equity playing field with students using social media and technology?
- ❖ What do you do to support students understanding the concepts of social justice and equity of opportunity?

Step Eight: Reparation

Reparation is seldom seen in models of cultural competency or proficiency. My hypothesis is that many academic researchers, counselors, and educators are focused on other aspects of creating competency within their respective professions. Although the social justice movement has been alive and well for several decades, mention of it as a foundation of cultural competence within a school context has only recently been noted.

Agarwal, Epstein, Oppenheim, Oyler, & Sonu write (2010),

The phrase *social justice* has proliferated in teacher education in recent years and is an umbrella term encompassing a large range of practices and perspective (Adams, Bell, & Griffin, 2006). These highlight the importance of multiple concepts, including but not limited to building classroom communities of dialogue across and with difference (Sapon-Shevin, 1999), critical multicultural and antibias education (Derman-Sparks & Ramsey, 2006), culturally relevant pedagogy (Ladson-Billings, 1994), culturally responsive and competent teachers (Irvine, 2003), antiracist teaching (Berlak & Moyenda, 2001), equity pedagogy (Banks & Banks, 1995), anti-oppressive teacher education (Kumashiro, 2004), disability rights (Linton, 1998), ableism (Hehir, 2002), and access to academics for students with disabilities (Kluth, Straut, & Biklen, 2003). There is an increasing number of books that are designed specifically for social justice-oriented teacher education building on the missions of teaching for social change (Darling-Hammond, French, & Garcia-Lopez, 2002), teaching and learning in a diverse world (Nieto, 2005) and critical social justice teacher education (Cochran-Smith, 2004). (p. 238)

Reparation is a large component of social justice and can be accomplished in a variety of ways. Volunteerism and mentoring can be viewed as a societal "give back," returning or restoring time and respect to a neighborhood but should always be done in deference to elders or leaders in the community. Asking, "What can I do?" and never saying, "Let me tell you what needs to be done" are important distinctions. Persistent yet respectful confrontation of prejudice is essential to reparation, so too, are apologies and making amends when and where appropriate.

During training workshops, the question I hear most often is this: *What do you do if a student calls you racist and you're not a racist?* This is often followed by, *The other (Black, Hispanic, Asian) kids don't think so!* I always ask, "How do you know the other kids don't think so?" and the answer is very often, *Because I ask them.* There are a great many problems with this, but I'm going to begin by answering the original question.

When a student calls us racist, there is only one thing to do: apologize. This is not only an issue of cultural consideration; it is an issue of good communication between human beings. If someone perceives that we have been unfair in any capacity, is our first response to say, "No; you're wrong"? Instead, in respectful communication, we apologize for any misunderstanding and we ask for clarification. At least that is the optimal response. (See Guidelines for Clear Communication, page 139.) Apologies are powerful. Apologies stop conflict in its tracks. There is little someone can do or say after an apology. Not only does it address what has been asserted (or alleged), but it also forces the person to either accept the apology and move on or expound on what underlying issues may be fueling the conflict.

The question, "What do you do if a student (or colleague) calls you racist?" comes up so frequently that I can almost predict the timing of it and it has allowed me to thoughtfully construct a series of interventive and instructive conversations. The question is, in fact, fundamental to the premise of cultural carelessness and insensitivity. Sometimes it is a function of color-blindness in the form of narcissistic altruism (see page 61).

Frankenberg (1997) along with Ladson-Billings (1994) discuss the "colorblind" position taken by many people whose initial recognition of privilege creates anxiety, guilt, and embarrassment. To cope with these feelings, it is not uncommon to adopt a position of neutrality which discounts cultural differences entirely.

"In a color-blind approach, there is a whole lot about a student you are not seeing. For example, saying 'I don't see a Mexican kid; I just see a kid,' you are preventing (knowledge) about that student's culture and community—and an important part of the student" (Sleeter, 2000/2001). When our first response is to defend ourselves and gather evidence rather than address the issue of racism or classism or sexism that someone has brought to us, we are dismissing the concerns of the other and declaring that our own honor and identity is more important.

The other issue at play in the assertion that "the other kids don't think I'm racist" is an assumption that all students of similar culture think and feel the same and therefore the stereotype that they all behave the same is not far behind. Cultural consideration and educational equity is foremost based upon individuality and individual experience. Maybe the other kids don't think a teacher is racist, but the one student who does is the one to whom we must attune our cultural antennae. Maybe the other kids are afraid to answer honestly because of the inherent power differential between teacher and student and/or white adult and child of color. Maybe the more important question could be: *Why does it bother me so much when a student tells me I'm racist?*

As with the legal terms of slander or defamation, responsibility for determining whether something is hurtful or harmful lies in the outcome to those who are the recipient of such terms. Dismissing a student's or colleague's assertion that something we say is culturally inconsiderate adds insult to injury. Like apologizing, acknowledging another's reality goes a very long way toward reducing cultural tensions.

Bonnie adds . . .

I respect and honor Kim's response to "What if someone calls you a racist?" And I feel I need to address the situation because there are high schools where students bandy about the term "racist" as often as they say "that's gay" and other demeaning and certainly not culturally considerate terms. This does not mean it is acceptable; it is not. I think we have to investigate deeply "what it looks like" when you call your teacher a racist or say something is "gay." We must continue to investigate the teacher behaviors that warranted the remark. And we have to assess the responses from peers after the remark was made. The teacher and the student and a counselor or mediator need to discuss the allegations. In preparation for this discussion, the teacher might ask herself: Do I have a solid relationship with this student? Would a student accuse me of being a racist if he felt he was learning in my class and not being left out or singled out unfairly? What were the actions that led up to his remark? What kind of response did he receive from peers after he called me a racist?

Scenario: Recently a superintendent in a district with 50% minority students, shared that a male student at the high school in her district would not stop calling his teachers racist. The teachers talked with him about this: the counselor talked with him; and the superintendent talked with the student to find out the "why" of the situation. They all came up with nothing. In the end, the superintendent believed the student was doing it to get out of doing his work by causing his teachers to feel guilty and to get attention from his peers.

With that conclusion, what would be your next steps as a culturally considerate educator? How might you continue courageous conversations about the situation? How can we make reparation to those we injure with our actions and our words?

Agarwal, Epstein, Oppenheim, Oyler, and Sonu (2010) assert that educators who teach for social justice (a) enact curricula that integrate multiple perspectives, questions dominant Western narratives, and are inclusive of the racial, ethnic, and linguistic diversity in North America; (b) support students to develop a critical consciousness of the injustices that characterize our society; and (c) scaffold opportunities for students to be active participants in a democracy, skilled in forms of civic engagement and deliberative discussion. These practices may challenge and alter an educational system that is not adequately serving large numbers of children, particularly poor children, children of color, and children with disabilities.

Britzman (2000) writes, "If teacher education is to join the world, be affected by its participation in world making, and question the 'goodness' of its own passions, we must rethink not only past practices and what goes on under the name of professionalism, but also the very imagination it will take to exceed compliance, fear of controversy, and 'unclaimed experiences.' Then, we might ask a new question: How does teacher education come to notice that the world matters?" (p. 204). The following example shows how one educator came to notice.

Twyla always joked about her name. Neither graceful nor agile as her mother had hoped when she named her after the acclaimed dancer and choreographer, Twyla had at least chosen an athletic profession. She was a physical education teacher and soccer coach. Twyla also joked about the remarks colleagues made, inferring the stereotype of lesbian gym teachers. These remarks were always in the guise of humor and Twyla laughed along. In fact, Twyla was married to Javier, a quiet and gentle man from Mexico who had two young sons. His first wife had died, and with help from his family, he raised his boys alone until his migration to the United States and marriage to Twyla.

I knew Twyla as a colleague. She was on the IEP team of a child I saw for therapy. We immediately hit it off. She was funny and insightful, and although she did not have a large role on the team, it was clear she had a large role in the life of our mutual student client. One day, after a meeting, she asked if she could call me regarding a personal matter. When she did call, I explained my steadfast boundaries about seeing colleagues in therapy, but as we talked, she explained that she understood and was really looking for a good referral. Would I be willing to talk with her and her husband about her oldest stepson, Joe? Joe was having problems with some of the kids at school. Maybe they could bring him in, too.

With some hesitation, I agreed. I liked Twyla and I also recognized the predicament of being a professional with a family issue playing out in one's work environment. In addition, Twyla found it especially difficult to help Joe because of the similar issues she was having with her own peers. While she could laugh off most of the comments, it was painful when Joe talked about being called derogatory names or accused of being "illegal." "I'm only eight!" he told Twyla. "How could I be a criminal?"

The comments about her sexual orientation "needled" Twyla, but the comments about her family's legal status and the racial slurs Joe reported seemed to bother her deeply. She had once overheard one of her students make a negative remark about her relationship with her husband, but this had confused her more than anything because the student was biracial and she thought he would be more understanding of her interracial marriage. When it came to her stepsons, however, she was extremely upset.

After conferring with Twyla, Javier, and Joe, I referred Joe to a child art therapist I respected. I also agreed to a time-limited professional development arrangement with Twyla which would involve helping her address the situations she was facing within her school in a positive and productive manner. It would not involve individual psychotherapy, and we agreed I would make another referral for her if we stumbled into deeper interpersonal issues.

Twyla was conflicted about how to handle concerns about Joe with the school because of her employment there. As a parent, she felt strongly that her son should be protected from negative comments and potential bullying by the other children. As a faculty member, she also knew the limitations of the school environment. "They are nice people," she would say, "but they aren't always very sensitive." Having been on an IEP team there, I knew exactly what she was talking about.

We discussed how to frame the problem clearly. How to make "I" statements, how to be specific about the incidents of homophobia directed at her, the racially charged ones Joe described, and how to share her own feelings of disappointment about her family being targeted in such a way. She listened but was uncharacteristically hesitant. She was an amiable woman, but not a timid one.

During one conversation, I suggested she say something very direct about her husband's immigration to the United States. "How about something like, 'Javier worked very hard to be a citizen of this country and it is disappointing to hear comments that undermine his commitment. I would like it if the students in Joe's class were educated about what his father did to become an American citizen and have it made clear that Joe is a citizen, too,'" I asked.

Twyla suddenly looked terrified and said, "I can't do that." It became clear that the situation was not only complicated but delicate. Javier was an undocumented immigrant. The boys had been brought to the United States after their mother died and they were undocumented as well. Twyla did not feel safe in confiding this information to anyone at her school and she found it difficult to know how to help her stepson respond when what the other kids were saying was basically true. Twyla would have overlooked my own inconsiderate assumption that Javier was naturalized, but after I apologized for my lack of sensitivity, I encouraged her to practice assertiveness with me by role playing how to state candidly that Javier's status was not the issue—respect of family's privacy and preservation of their human dignity was.

In my experience, the issue of immigration—documented or otherwise—is one of the fastest growing in education and particularly in my state. African American students still are the subject of many comments about why test scores are below average and classroom behavior is poor. Increasingly, however, it is "those ELL kids" who frustrate teachers and are thought to be the cause of swelling class sizes.

Recently, a culturally sensitive educator told me how difficult it was for her to know that her school's budget did not permit the purchase of a $15,000 trailer to augment the limited school building in response to the sudden influx of students, but the district could spend ten times that on resodding the football field at another school. "The administration actually said out loud that it wasn't worth the money because there was no guarantee those kids would be here next year. How is that putting the kids first?"

This is not a forum for immigration, but it is one for illustration of how quality education is intertwined with social justice and equality. If one child or one group of children is excluded from the opportunity to learn in a comfortable classroom or receive a culturally conscientious curriculum, all children are at risk. This is the message which can reach beyond margins and marginalized populations. If a school or district is able to discount the need of one child because of invisibility, lack of cultural awareness, or fiscal excuse, that school or district is capable of discounting the need of any child at any time.

Britzman (2000) asked, "How does teacher education come to notice that the world matters?" Twyla was virtually unaware of the issues faced by immigrants or English language learners until she married Javier. She was the first to admit that before Joe began having problems, the full scope of the issues did not occur to her. She had never really understood the consequences to children or the meaning of the Dream Act (National Immigration Law Center, 2011) until she felt their impact personally.

Bonnie writes about Reparation

Britzman asks, "How can teacher education come to notice that the world matters?" I must ask, as a teacher educator, how can I ensure I support teachers in learning about the worlds their students inhabit and they inhabit? Kim says I don't come to this work from a viewpoint of social justice; no, I did not call it that, but from my earliest memories, I wanted to "save the world." When anyone asked me what I wanted to do with my life from third grade through high school, it was to work with the people of New Guinea. Early on, I saw social justice as missionary work; then I grew to understand it was not my place to decide who and how one should be changed. Instead, I needed to learn and understand that others learn in their own ways, and I needed to make reparation for past mistakes in the best ways I could.

Reparation feels like such a strong word to place into a model of cultural consideration, yet so fitting. If we truly need to make reparations for past mistakes, how exactly can we do this? There is no exact way. There are many ways. Find ways that best fit your passion and your work.

How do I make reparation? I do it by and through the work. I continue to learn "what I don't know I don't know" and then work to rectify the wrongs I have committed. I do it by employing an empathetic mind and spirit as I go about my daily life. I do it by practicing the daily reflections Kim suggests.

What are examples of reparation you practice?

As we work together to create culturally considerate schools, how might we support educators who enter classrooms filled with few or many students who are culturally different from them and who wonder if they need to do anything differently? These might be

- ❖ teachers who wonder if they need to do something different, and if so, then how might they do it;
- ❖ teachers who want to address any of this—but don't have the tools to begin the journey;
- ❖ teachers who believe they are good people (and they are) yet find it challenging to bring up issues of culture and participate in discussions surrounding culture;
- ❖ teachers who have not had the opportunity to observe the discrimination, all the while assuming they understand others' realities and experiences;
- ❖ white female teachers who, perhaps, do not understand white privilege (see page 62) and who need tools to examine white female culture as it impacts their classroom management and instruction;
- ❖ white male teachers who do not understand the influence of white privilege and patriarchy as it impacts students and how it may influence student achievement;

❖ teachers who do *not* want to address any of this—who say they do not see color or culture (see "color-blindness" page 96) and they treat all children the same;

❖ teachers who don't accept the nonclosure of dealing with issues of culture and teachers who don't want to participate in discussions surrounding culture;

❖ teachers who have had limited experience with other cultures and find it difficult to develop empathy for them.

Yes, discrimination still occurs. I fight daily my racist biases. In workshops, I offer examples of my own thoughts—call them racist or biased or stereotypical—but they are thoughts I continue to fight. For example, while on a treadmill in a hotel in Omaha, Nebraska, I noticed a woman who appeared about my age walk by with cleaning supplies, clearly a woman who was there to clean rooms. Looking at her, I thought, "I can't believe this woman is still cleaning toilets at my age (64)... and she's even white!" When I ask participants in workshops to discuss what they had just heard, they say things such as, "It's classist because you don't think cleaning toilets is as honorable a job as what you do." They say, "It's sexist because you don't think women should be the ones cleaning toilets." And they say, "It's racist because you assume only Women of Color are the ones who clean toilets in hotel rooms."

We discuss all of these assumptions, and I share with them that I believe I would not have noticed that woman had she been a Woman of Color. I believe I would have gone on watching the morning news on the television set overhead. But because I confronted my assumption by seeing an older, white cleaning woman, I was able to reflect upon my stereotypical, classist, sexist, racist bias. Then I ask myself, "How does this subconscious belief carry over into the classroom where I teach or into the workshop or into my daily interaction with other human beings?"

I must continually challenge myself: When a white man walks into the room with a woman of color, do I assume the man is the superintendent and the woman of color is a principal? Do I continue to assume the person of authority is the white person, no matter what the situation? People of Color tell me this happens to them often. They are automatically assumed by others to hold the less prestigious position. Can I explain this away by referring to my past and the number of incidences that reaffirm my expectations and my biases? How do we talk about this with each other? And when we do, how do we communicate showing respect and honoring the journey of each individual involved yet move the conversation along the path to social justice?

Reflections/Questions

❖ What do you do to challenge your classroom assumptions and ensure you are making reparation in the form of equitable instruction for all students?

❖ How do you engage in conversation with yourself and with your colleagues to uncover how and where you can make reparation for past wrongdoings to others?

❖ Give examples of how you "pay it forward" in the areas of social justice and equity.

❖ What goals can you set for yourself as you plan to make reparation and continue your journey of cultural consideration?

Reparation extends to all stakeholders, district administration and school boards as well as classroom teachers, coaches, and principals. In the December 13, 2010, issue of *Newsweek*, Michelle Rhee wrote openly and honestly about how she could have communicated better during her tenure as chancellor of the Washington, DC, public school system—a public act of reparation.

"I could have done a better job of communicating. I did a particularly bad job letting the many good teachers know that I considered them to be the most important part of the equation. I should have said to the effective teachers, 'You don't have anything to worry about. My job is to make your life better, offer you more support, and pay you more.' I totally fell down on doing that." Rhee also owns her inability to communicate effectively with parents. "I didn't do enough to bring [them] along, either . . . We didn't connect the dots for them."

Michelle Rhee notes that laws and policies are made through the exertion of influence, writing, "Powerful interests put pressure on our elected officials and government institutions to sway or stop change."

Education is no different . . . You can see the impact of this dynamic playing out every day. Policymakers, school district administrators, and school boards who are beholden to special interests have created a bureaucracy that is focused on the adults instead of the students. Go to any public school board meeting in the country and you'll rarely hear the words "children," "students," or "kids" uttered. Instead, the focus remains on what jobs, contracts, and departments are getting which cuts, additions, or changes. The rationale for the decisions mostly rests on which grown-ups will be affected, instead of what will benefit or harm children. (Rhee, 2010)

Rhee states that the teachers' unions get the blame for much of this but doesn't feel that the unions can or should change, writing, "The purpose of the teachers' union is to protect the privileges, priorities, and pay of their members." She asserts that it falls upon the educational reform community to exert influence as well and has started StudentsFirst, a national movement to transform public education, its mission being to defend and promote the interests of children so that America has the best education system in the world (Rhee, 2010).

Cultural Considerations
for Equity and Social Justice

- Now that you have read the chapters of this book, reassess your cultural awareness as first suggested on page 25. Define the terms "culture" and "cultural consideration" for yourself. List five things that make you a culturally considerate teacher. List five improvements you already know you could make toward increasing your cultural consideration. Writing to our own prompts reflects we are working on a deeper level and beginning to understand what we don't know we don't know and better identify those things we do know in order to build upon them.

- Assess yourself for culturally relevant instruction. Choose one culturally relevant strategy to implement, and self-assess your implementation over a two-week period. Record your findings in your journal.

- Assess the community in your classroom for culturally considerate interactions. Ask students to write culturally considerate actions on a sticky note and post them on a bulletin board. Even though this may seem trivial and superficial, it can build awareness of actions we need to take and to develop in our students.

- Keep a gratitude journal. Ask students to think of one thing they are grateful for and record it in their daily journal. Model this by recording your own and sharing with students. (See page 121 for Kim's *Inward Bound* model.)

- Build a cadre of colleagues for equity coaching. Observe and give feedback to each other. Examine student data to inform your practice and give evidence of equity. Where inequities exist, discuss how you might together work to eradicate them through culturally relevant practices.

PART III

Educating Without Bias

9

Portraits of Culturally Considerate Educators

Bonnie writes . . .

Throughout the book, Kim has offered research for creating Culturally Considerate schools as well as her personal and professional knowledge. My contribution has been both personal and professional but always written from the perspective of a teacher. Even though you have read educator portraits earlier in the book, in this chapter, you will find additional portraits of educators currently working in today's schools. Before beginning, imagine your ideal Culturally Considerate educator; what does he or she look like in action?

Portraits of Cultural Consideration

A high school history teacher begins his class with a quiet, calm statement. He is dressed in a suit and tie, his daily uniform. (He tells me he is one of the few Latino teachers in the building and knows he is a role model.) He tells the students exactly what they will be learning that day (the standard is also posted clearly on the board). He requires students repeat it back to him in a choral fashion. He uses a warm-up that ties directly to the concepts he intends to teach. He uses nonverbal signals throughout the class; he uses humor appropriately; he is playful but serious; the students stay engaged. He gets a male student to move from a back seat to a front seat without stopping his instruction, then engages the student. His classroom is filled with visuals of role models from a variety of cultures as well as charts, student pictures, sports information, and other visuals that relate to the students. He integrates student movement flawlessly into the room filled with 42 bodies. He does mini-lectures, peppering his lecture with personal references to his students' lives and throwing in a few Spanish words and phrases. He uses analogies to student lives to illustrate his major points. He has students process the information and share with others. He salvaged old white tiles to use as response boards for his students so he can continually check for understanding. He includes a creative activity to deepen the understanding of the material. He concludes with "check-out" slips to monitor understanding.

The following are practices the teacher uses in his classroom:

- ❖ The teacher tells the students exactly what they will be learning that day.
- ❖ The warm-up ties directly to the lesson.
- ❖ The teacher uses humor appropriately.
- ❖ The teacher uses a pair/share discussion of the material.
- ❖ The teacher uses a visual timer for discussion, reflection, and other work.
- ❖ The teacher uses graphic organizers.
- ❖ The teacher uses nonverbal commands.
- ❖ The teacher uses direct verbal commands.
- ❖ The teacher uses innovative materials.
- ❖ The teacher uses proximity.
- ❖ The teacher connects to students' lives with the content.
- ❖ The teacher holds high expectations.
- ❖ The teacher has outstanding classroom management.
- ❖ The teacher has students working with others.
- ❖ The teacher has students working at higher levels, ending with a creative activity to embed the learning.

Several students who were interviewed said this teacher was their favorite. It was easy to see why. Respect oozed from him. His classroom was quiet and respectful even though the school sat in an area known for its gangs and violence. After class, students were asked what they liked about the class and the teacher. Below are two responses from students in this teacher's class.

"Mr. G. is a great teacher because he understands us all. He knows where we need help. He teaches us like he was one of us. There might be a lot of people in this class, but he always seems to have time for every single one of us if we need help. You got to respect us if you want to receive it."

"Mr. G. is a great teacher. He helps students where they are in need of help. He always has a positive attitude and always respects the students. Most teachers don't understand that. Mr. G. understands that you have to have a good attitude and respect to receive it from the students."

Time and time again, the students state that they like a teacher when the teacher demands they do the work and helps them when they need help. Finally, they almost always bring up the R-word: Respect.

This in no way is a comprehensive description of best practices; however, it is a small vignette of powerful strategies teachers can use to show respect and honor for their students. Our students are the future, and unless we can understand what respect means to them and show them that respect, we diminish our ability as an effective teacher who supports all students to achieve at high levels.

Mr. Kellogg: Ninth-Grade Study Skills Teacher

Chelsea explains why Mr. Kellogg is her favorite teacher: "He makes the class interesting, and we still learn." Chelsea shared how Mr. Kellogg shares his own experiences with the ninth-grade students in a study skills class. He grew up in poverty and lost his mother when he was a teen. He was homeless for a while and never thought he would make it to college and become a teacher. But he persisted, and with the support of others, he made it. Now Mr. Kellogg connects with his students in this high-poverty school, and he tells them they, too, can make it through high school and college. He is passionate about giving back to students so they can achieve in life.

Ms. Jones: Assistant Principal

Ms. Jones is an assistant principal at an urban high school in the Los Angeles area. She attended K–12 in the district and is aware of the strengths and challenges of the staff and students. Biracial, she identifies as African American, and she is the only full-time African American female in the building. She reflects daily about her role at the school and is insistent about providing an equitable setting for the students in her school. Even though the high school has nearly 1,000 students, Ms. Jones knows each student by name and can connect them to their families and community. Having engaged in self-examination throughout her adolescence and early adulthood, Ms. Jones is aware of her racial identity and how she interacts with others. She does have a bias. She is strongly biased against any staff member who believes any one of these children is incapable of learning at high levels and of achieving competency of core standards. Not afraid to face teachers' lack of expectations for the student population, Ms. Jones confronts staff about their biases and challenges them to improve on their equity skills.

Ms. Lepperson: Principal

Ms. Lepperson is the principal of an elementary school in a district in North Carolina known for its high test scores and outstanding education.

Yet Ms. Lepperson sees inequities in the school where she has recently become principal. She sets out on a journey to change the culture of the school from one that tends to be elitist and exclusive to one that is inclusive and responsive to all children. In her school, there are significant populations of special education students, ELL students, and refugee population students. Ms. Lepperson knows she must support the teachers in reaching all the students. She begins by providing professional development in areas of equity. Using the Culturally Considerate Model, she guides her staff through Self-Examination and has them keep journals in which they record their experiences. They share these at team meetings and staff meetings, and they set goals for their continued work. Ms. Lepperson brings in presenters from different cultural backgrounds from the staff, including different religions, sexual identities, and racial identities. These presenters lead the staff through various exercises which stretch their thinking and support their better understanding their cultural lens. Ms. Lepperson has a therapist who teaches the staff how to use cognitive restructuring in order to change thinking patterns. She exposes them to new information about the cultures of the students in the school. She brings in experts in culturally responsive teaching, and the teachers practice new strategies and do peer observations. Afterward, they dialogue in learning communities about next steps. Finally, Ms. Lepperson offers options for staff to practice reparation in the forms of volunteerism.

These educators illustrate Culturally Considerate pedagogy through their instruction and behaviors. How do they align with what you imagined as a model of a Culturally Considerate Educator?

Bonnie asks: How do you create culturally considerate instruction? How do you ensure equal access to content knowledge?

Over the past years, I have been in hundreds of teachers' classrooms in districts across the country. Some districts are part of an equity project focused on supporting teachers as they implement classroom strategies to culturally connect to student lives. These teachers work hard to connect with a variety of student cultures: adolescent, gender, ethnic, class, gang, or others. The most successful teachers are those who know their subject matter and consistently, carefully, and considerately connect the academic content to their students' lives through examples, stories, metaphors, analogies, and interactive activities. Whether the discipline is physics, history, biology, English, Spanish, or math, the content they teach must be relevant to the students' lives in order to engage them. In *The Highly Engaged Classroom*, Robert Marzano poses four questions for teachers as they examine their instruction: How do I feel? Is it interesting? Is it important? Can I do it? By using Marzano's questions, teachers can reflect upon individual students and discover what is standing in the way of the student learning new concepts, placing them in working memory, and ultimately embedding them into long term memory (Marzano & Pickering, 2011).

As teachers reflect upon these questions, they need to consider the following:

❖ Do the teachers really know what the students' lives are like? Have they driven by the homes of the students or visited families in their homes?

❖ Do they understand the roles that institutions—churches and community organizations—play in the lives of the students?

❖ Do they know and understand the gang culture and how it affects their students? Do they understand other peer cultures of their students?

❖ Do the teachers understand the brain research to know the importance of making the connections from the content material to students' lives and can they articulate that to their students? Students are usually interested in their own brains; why not share this information about how the brain works with the students using a model of a brain and some basic facts and examples?

❖ Do the teachers know and understand their content well enough—to the point of automaticity—to be able to think metaphorically and make connections to students' lives?

❖ Do the teachers work in a climate where they can share ideas and formulate ways to make important connections for their students to their content? Are there Professional Learning Communities centered on content disciplines as well as other professional issues?

If teachers can answer "yes" to most of the above, they have a greater opportunity for creating a culturally considerate classroom where respect is practiced by each individual in the room.

10

Landscape of a Culturally Considerate School

Aculturally considerate school is rich with culturally conscientious educators who inspire students and their families, staff
and colleagues, individual schools, and school districts to be at their
best each and every day. Bonnie and I both had the accidental honor
of knowing one such educator.

As a speech and language specialist for the St. Louis Special
School District, Richard Ashburner was a colleague of Bonnie's for
many years. I knew Richard socially through a group of friends and
extended family who sing in the chorus of the St. Louis Symphony
Orchestra. Recently, Richard passed away suddenly after a brief illness, leaving a trail of grace and gratitude far longer than the grief
experienced in the quake of his death.

Megan Denall, former Coordinator, St. Louis Symphony Orchestra
Community Partnership and Education Program, spoke at his memo-
rial and said this:

> Richard served as a consultant for the Symphony's education
> department, lending his expertise in education, professional
> development, and program design to lead us in an in-depth

effort to revamp our in-school programs. Before our collaborations with Richard, our programs always seemed to miss the mark. After eight years of his gentle guidance, we fully realize that student behavior was *not* the issue. *Our* behavior was the source of the problem. We needed a new educational philosophy, one that placed our focus on what we wanted students to know and be able to do. We needed lesson designs that incorporated differentiated instruction, positive behavior supports, and a variety of learning modalities so that every student in the classroom felt as though our programs were designed just for them.

Where Richard's gifts as a communicator and mentor really came into play was in coaching sessions with musicians. After observing programs in the classroom, Richard and the ensemble would meet to reflect upon the lesson. Richard's attention to detail meant that every moment of the program was timed. When the musicians [recognized] that a certain part of the program felt uncomfortable, Richard could tell them the exact minute it happened and how students were reacting [or not reacting] in that moment. But Richard was not dictatorial in his guidance. As [members of the orchestra] shared with me, Richard had a generosity of spirit in sharing his expertise, every detail, every transition, every visual aid was important because it made a difference to students . . . Richard was able to teach how the mind of a child works and therefore how best to reach out to them in a way that could captivate and interest them in music [and has] changed how [we] approach all different audiences . . . each performance situation as a learning opportunity for those listening and try to figure out how best to capture their attention in a meaningful way. Richard never took himself too seriously but always gave great advice and support, a fantastic combination . . . He was a fantastic educator of educators, such an amazing quality!!

What is a culturally considerate school? It is a school rich with Richards who orchestrate beautiful lessons for their classrooms and support the solo voice of each student. While each school will be distinct from every other school, depending upon the makeup of its students, the community in which it operates, and the different personalities working within its walls, there are a few features which must exist in order for a culturally considerate atmosphere to thrive. A culturally considerate school

- Demonstrates awareness of the many cultures represented within the school community
- Gives voice and consideration to all students
- Welcomes all types of families
- Shows interest, empathy, and respect for each faculty and staff member
- Advocates respect and reverence of individuality
- Acknowledges limitations in resources and puts forth efforts to fill needs
- Admits mistakes and changes policy, programs, and personnel accordingly
- Adapts innovative policies in the interest of the total school community—even when uncomfortable or unpopular

A culturally considerate school demonstrates awareness of the many cultures represented within the school community in a variety of ways. Perhaps most important is that many different cultures are represented within the faculty, staff, and administration. A diverse faculty exposes students to differing teaching styles, personal attitudes, and varying behaviors. A diverse administration gives credence to the fact anyone can succeed and decisions are not all made by a white, heterocentric, physically abled male majority.

The implementation of curricula, textbooks, lessons, and classroom activities which denote difference and diversity is likewise critical to demonstrating a school's commitment to cultural consideration. Balanced and inclusive literature, social science materials, and hard science examples which incorporate resources from all walks of life give students choices of study which speak to their personal experiences.

The presence of multicultural media in classrooms and in the school library are critical to making all students feel welcome as is the type of media displayed around the school building. Posters, fliers, books, pamphlets, photographs, and artwork need to reflect the population of the school, but also include populations which are not yet represented within the current school demographics. Giving the message that everyone not only *is* but *will be* welcome into the school community allows students, families, staff, and educators all to feel freer to disclose important identities they may have previously felt necessary to keep secret.

A culturally considerate school gives voice and consideration to all students by genuinely requesting input from every student at frequent intervals. At times this can be anonymous; at other times, inviting students to conduct a performance evaluation on the school can be extremely helpful. It is important to assure and *in*sure each student that there will be no consequences for negative comments or poor evaluations. In some cases, gently guiding students to learn the fine art of constructive criticism may be necessary, but it is important to make that secondary to truly hearing a student if he or she has concerns or frustrations.

All types of families are welcome at culturally considerate schools. Single-parent families, blended families, multiracial families, gay and lesbian parents, differently abled parents, and families that practice faiths which are unfamiliar all must be treated with the same visible level of dignity and respect. Not only does this allow each student to feel pride in and acceptance of his or her own family, but it also models how people of difference can communicate clearly and conscientiously.

Likewise, a culturally considerate school models positive regard by showing interest, empathy, and respect for each faculty and staff member. When students see educators treating one another kindly and with patience, even when there are distinctions or disagreements, they learn consideration by example.

A culturally considerate school advocates respect and reverence of individuality. This may sometimes push limits and boundaries of school policies—and sometimes the buttons of administration and faculty—but students need to feel safe to express themselves openly and without restriction unless there is risk of mortal harm to self or others.

Culturally considerate schools acknowledge limitations in resources and put forth efforts to fill needs. In these economically challenged times, this may seem like a tall order, but it is also a call to find creative solutions to deficit thinking. No student should do without necessary educational tools or environmental safety because of budgetary concerns. When a student hears that their needs cost too much, he or she actually hears, "you're not worth it," and we must be able to admit, on some level, this is precisely what we are saying.

A culturally considerate school admits mistakes and changes policy, programs, and personnel accordingly. Of all the traits of a school without bias, this is probably the most difficult to achieve. History, ego, and legalities are just a few of the many reasons change is slow to come to some schools and school districts. As society, communities, and student populations shift, however, educational change is inevitable—and unavoidable. *Apologies are a magic elixir for relationships . . .* (Bloom, 2008). Perhaps not magic, but admitting mistakes, making changes, and discharging incompetent personnel are rescue remedies for stressed and beleaguered schools.

When adapting innovative policies in the interest of the total school community—even when uncomfortable or unpopular—a school proves itself to be culturally conscious of the needs of all students, families, faculty, staff, and administrators. Making change is one thing. Making change in the wake of discomfort or controversy is courageous. Increasingly, schools are stepping up to the challenge by encouraging self-examination, reflection, integration, and actualization which lead to educational equity and social justice.

PART IV

Appendices & Tools

Worksheets

In the following pages, we have provided the worksheets we introduced within the book, supplemental self-care information, and a list of resources for continued personal and professional growth. We are happy to share these with you. Much of the material is original and/or copyrighted so we also would appreciate appropriate credit if you copy and distribute them within your professional learning communities.

You will find

- Inward Bound: A Wholistic Plan for Body, Mind, Psyche, and Spirit
- Scenarios to Study
- Wholistic Reflection Worksheet
- Cultural Consideration Event Summary
- Personal Rights
- Guidelines for Clear Communication
- Emotions/Feelings and Body Signal List
- Cultural Awareness Matrix
- Rules of Engagement
- Conflict Resolution
- Problem Solving Steps
- Culturally Considerate Resources

Inward Bound

Inward Bound (Anderson, 1996, 1999, 2001, 2011) is a wholistic wellness practice for mind, body, psyche, and spirit, all of which are important to wholistic wellness. Thinking clearly, identifying feelings (body and emotion), integration of what is known at one's core, and a sense of connectedness are all important factors in healing and in physical and mental health. Establishing a daily wellness practice to address each of these important aspects of the self is essential. They may feel awkward, irritating, or time-consuming at first, but once integrated into daily life, these practices can become second nature.

Sunrise Pages

This practice is similar to Julia Cameron's morning pages in that she suggests writing Morning Pages as a way to begin rediscovering the creative process, but also as a way to release thoughts and feelings that are barriers to creativity. In the context of Inward Bound, we use Sunrise Pages as a psychic constitutional—a healthy way to purge mental and emotional toxins through a brief free write.

Soon after you awake in the morning, sit down with pen and paper and write nonstop for five minutes. Use an egg timer or your phone. Don't use a computer; the physical act of writing is important. Don't stop writing until the five minutes are up, even if you repeat yourself or write nonsense words. When you are finished, do not read what you have written. Close the tablet, put the pages in a folder, or store them in a drawer. You are done with your morning pages and it's time to move on.

Daily Intention

Setting an intention for each day is a simple way to begin discovering purpose. Intentions can be as general as "It will be a good day today," or as specific as "I will find three things of beauty today." At first, it may be necessary to set an intention such as "I will not use derogatory slang today" but soon that can be amended to a positive statement and become, "I will treat my colleagues with respect today." Write your intention on a small piece of paper and put it in a pocket. If things begin to feel out of balance, take the paper out and read your intention aloud three times.

Food Plan

A food plan is just that—a plan for food. There are no bad foods but sometimes people don't make the best choices about food due to the lack of planning. Food plans help to take the mystery and sometimes evil magic out of food intake and assist in overall physical and emotional health by setting food intention. It is often random or responsive eating that becomes problematic.

Movement

Thirty minutes of low impact aerobic movement daily helps keep the body flexible and endorphins flowing which are extremely important in sustaining wellness. Depression and stress generate both mental and physical exhaustion, and pharmacological research now has caught up to what psychotherapists have known for years—depression and stress cause pain and jeopardize immune function. The release of endorphins reduces pain, strengthens the immune system, and offsets other symptoms such as sleep disturbance, appetite changes, lack of focus, and energy depletion.

Affirmations

Affirming the positive in one's life is a manifestation of our wellness foundation. Stating out loud or writing statements that affirm what is good and true may bring to mind an old *Saturday Night Live* skit, but the eventual impact on self-concept and confidence is serious business. As with intentions, begin with short and simple statements: *I can do this. I am intelligent. My body is strong. I am a caring person.*

Twilight Pages

Nighttime is often difficult for people in the throes of emotional challenges or work overload. Not only is the dark and quiet unsettling, but biorhythms may either begin to wane or in some instances, an individual body clock may be in contradiction to the rest of the world. Establishing an evening routine is probably one of the most important components of health and wellness.

Twilight pages are much like sunrise pages in that they are designed to collect thoughts and feelings and set them aside, however in this instance, the positive and productive portions of the day are collected, put out onto paper with pen in hand, and gently tucked away.

Set your timer for five minutes (soon you won't need a timer—you'll just know when to stop and start) and begin to write about the accomplishments of the day. Don't let your hand stop writing. When the five minutes are up, stop. This time, take three deep, cleansing breaths, and walk around the room for another five minutes. Come back to the twilight pages and read them. Take three more cleansing breaths and give thanks for fulfilling your day's intention by making an offering to your gratitude grotto.

Gifts of Gratitude

Whether it is a grotto, altar, treasure chest, or shoe box, craft a receptacle for symbols of gratitude. Becoming aware of gratitude in our lives takes us beyond pain and frustration and brings us out into the world where goodness survives amidst tragedy and freedom exists after oppression.

Each night, create a symbol of something for which you are grateful. It can be anything: a poem, a drawing, a clipping from a magazine, a rock, a puff of cat fur. It needs to be tangible—something you can see and touch, hear or smell. The senses must be involved so that you can fully take in the significance of the person or event for which you are grateful.

Deposit your symbol into your gratitude chest. These tangible objects will be there for a rainy day when it might be more difficult to find a rosebud for which to be thankful.

Centering Before Bedtime

Western medicine calls it "sleep hygiene." Zen Buddhists will not call it anything as *sleep is what it is and does what it does.* But a few things will help increase the odds of a good night's sleep.

- Establish a regular sleep routine and time.
- Create a pleasant sleep space which takes all senses into account.
- Reduce all other sensory stimulation at least one hour before bed.
- If you are prone to bad dreams or nightmares, understand that this is information for growth, not to terrorize. Nightmares will subside when they are embraced and the lessons they bring are learned.
- Associate your sleep space with sleep—not watching TV or doing work or homework.
- Be comfortable when you get into bed. Wear PJs which are soft and not binding. If a new mattress is not in your budget, maybe a foam topper or new pillows are.
- Center yourself by taking deep, relaxing breaths.
- Affirm that you will sleep and sleep peacefully. Welcome the information dreams may have for you but ask that it come gently so you may listen and learn.

Along with these daily practices, the following facets of day-to-day life need to be carefully and considerately attended.

Connecting with Family and Friends

Human connection is vital to becoming a vital human being. Sometimes it is necessary to find a new circle of friends or adopt an extended family, but it is a necessary part of health and healing. Trust cannot be rebuilt or newly discovered without having people to push against and pull toward us.

Education, Vocation, Avocation

Finding a "right livelihood" brings self-esteem and builds self-confidence. Whether it is finishing another degree or getting the job of your dreams, finding an environment in which you feel comfortable and respected is important. It is likewise important that you respect your colleagues. Unfortunately money is necessary, though not evil as the often misquoted adage states. But money must be secondary to comfort or the likelihood of joblessness increases.

Creation

Everyone has the capacity to create. Creativity is not a gift bestowed upon the deserving. It is a human quality. We may not be able to draw as well as another person or sing our way to stardom, but we can create. There are many vehicles that are rarely considered for creative transportation of our thoughts and feelings. In addition to the "fine" arts, sewing, gardening, carpentry, cooking, or rebuilding cars may be your vehicle of choice. Don't diminish anything you create.

Nurture Something

Closely aligned to creation, nurturing a pet, a plant, or a talent validates our stamina. Yes, as educators and helpers we nurture each day, but nurturing something unrelated to our jobs shows that we can see things through without a paycheck to prompt us. We can grow.

Recreation

Have fun! All work—internal and external—and no play makes for a tired and resentful person. Activities must simply be fun for the sake of fun—not purposeful. Fun has no purpose other than to invoke joy and happiness. It may take a few tries and trying new things, but recreation is just as important as any other column on the healing chart.

Helping Others, Giving Back

Bonnie and I feel very strongly about Reparation as an important step toward Equity and Social Justice. I also feel it is an important part of personal growth. It may seem overwhelming to help others when we give at the office each day, but stepping outside of our comfort zone to make someone else more comfortable gives perspective and a sense of accomplishment that is unsurpassed. Some ideas are volunteering at a community garden, tutoring new immigrants in English, cooking or serving food for those in need, building houses with an organization like Habitat for Humanity. Efforts do not have to be organized. Watering an ailing neighbor's lawn or taking pets to the vet for an elderly or physically challenged person can be just as rewarding. Set a limit of time devoted to your efforts each week. Balance in all things, even volunteerism.

Spiritual Practice

Faith or belief does not have to mean organized religion or naming a deity, but becoming reacquainted with a sense of something beyond ourselves can give purpose and direction. For those who identify as agnostic or atheist, this may seem culturally insensitive. Though that is not my intention, I acknowledge the contradiction. The truth is, I have never found alternative verbiage that didn't sound awkward or pandering to me.

Connecting with Nature

Connecting with Nature can be grounding, calming, and can assist in becoming more connected to one's body and inner voice of reason. Make outings as simple as possible. Carry little with you. Return with less. Breathe deeply. Walk gently. Attune to the sounds. Quiet time in Nature can stand alone as a meditation.

Scenarios to Study

The following are scenarios educators might encounter each day, examples of questions that arise, and responses to consider. An educator supplied the scenarios. We asked the questions and suggested interventions. Consider taking these to your next PLC meeting and discussing with colleagues.

Scenario No. 1

Staff members who have worked together for years, for the most part, have not acknowledged their bias. They spent the year reading culturally aware texts such as Courageous Conversations. Group members are hesitant to discuss openly their feelings and openly acknowledge their bias. They fear seeming racist in front of the two African American women who participate in the group.

Questions:

1. With whom have they discussed these issues if not in open forums?

2. What makes them fear seeming racist?

3. How would they describe the bias they do acknowledge?

4. What do they anticipate will happen if they do discuss these feelings in front of their colleagues of color?

Considerations:

When we deliberately withhold information from those affected by that knowledge, we are making a choice to segregate ourselves from the whole. In turn, in doing this, we don't allow others to make decisions or act based upon fact.

There is a difference between "privacy" and "secrecy." Privacy is a choice and does not adversely affect anyone else. Secrecy is generally held out of fear of consequence or reprisal. Privacy is a right when practiced properly. Secrecy is most often self-serving, destructive, and unnecessary. Secrets also often have a way of slithering out when least expected, causing far more damage than any honest disclosure or confrontation ever could.

Interventions:

This scenario would take us back to the first two stages in the Model of Cultural Consideration and Equity Skill Building. Self-Examination and Reflection would be necessary to ever move this staff toward a higher level of educational equity. Suggested interventions:

❖ Establish Rules of Engagement (page 138) and review Guidelines for Clear Communication (page 139) before any group task or process.
❖ Ask the staff to complete the Cultural Self-Awareness Matrix (according to the guidelines outlined on page 76) and engaging in small group discussions regarding individual discoveries of themselves and others.
❖ Ask staff members to move into dyads with the person they know best in the room. Without sharing with one another, ask that each person write down five adjectives to describe the other.
  o Now ask staff members to move into dyads with someone they know least. Again, without sharing with one another, ask that each person write down five adjectives to describe the other.
  o Ask whether participants feel comfortable sharing either list with their dyadic partner. If so, ask that they do so. If not, ask that they spend five to ten minutes reflecting upon why they do not feel comfortable.
  o When reflective time has passed, urge each reluctant person to *take a chance for change* (see page 62) and share one of the five adjectives with the group at large.
  o With the Guidelines for Clear Communication in mind, ask the person described by the adjective to respond.
  o Encourage the group as a whole to discuss their thoughts, feelings, knowledge, and beliefs (page 89) about the process.

Scenario No. 2

The teacher is a white female in her fifties. She is in her final years of teaching and is determined to do a good job. She has attended many diversity trainings and she has acknowledged her bias and assessed her equity skills. She believes she understands her strengths and limitations. However, she has a male biracial student she is unable to reach. He is an extremely creative student, and he is in her creative writing class. He is sporadic in his production of writing for her, and he is in danger of failing and not graduating as a result of failing the class. Since this high school has a conference writing program, she has several opportunities to work with him one-on-one in privacy, and she tried hard to reach him and convince him to do his work. She has allowed him latitude in the parameters of assignments. She is very frustrated and does not know what to do.

Questions:

1. Does this teacher assume that she is unable to help this student because he is biracial?

   a. If so, why?

2. Has she consulted with other faculty members about his performance in their classes?

3. Has she talked with the school counselor about any family or emotional challenges he may be having?

4. Has she referred him for testing?

Considerations:

Going by this information alone, it would seem that the teacher may be hypersensitive to the boy's racial makeup to the exclusion of other possible factors. Being a culturally considerate educator includes taking ethnographic elements into account, but does not assume they are the sole cause for all academic achievement concerns.

This may be an example of "narcissistic altruism" (see page 61). Sometimes the more we know, the less we listen. Seasoned professionals in the field of education and diversity can be the most challenging when it comes to equity skill building. If an educator specializes in special education, he or she may see intellectual differences before other causes for a student's struggle. The school counselor may see emotional or mental health problems. If a teacher has specific interest and credentialing in diversity or multicultural issues, he or she may look for cultural reasons in situations where there may be other more pressing reasons for a student's performance or behavior.

Paradoxically, by unnecessarily focusing on cultural issues, the issue of culture DOES become an issue. Cultural consideration and educational equity mean a holistic view of all students, taking into account all facets of a child or adolescent's heritage, history, geographic origin, circumstances, and relational bonds (page 65).

Interventions:

❖ Assign a literacy coach to the classroom to help assess the progress of all students. Make every attempt to assign a coach of color to this classroom. Do not call attention to the student in question, but do pay attention to the coach's notes about him.

❖ Ask the teacher to join a professional learning community (PLC) in order to receive peer support and supervision for all of her students.

❖ Invite all students to "grade" their teachers for cultural consideration. See if anything stands out from the evaluations given by the students of this teacher.

   o If student responses are in contradiction to the teacher's self-perception, share this information with the teacher in a clear and respectful manner. Ask her to participate in professional development programs to "refresh" her skills.

   o If the teacher's grades match her beliefs about her cultural aptitude, share the information with her and her students. Remember that silence does not necessarily mean agreement.

   o If there have been a few evaluations that do not seem to agree with a positive assessment, invite those students to give specific, personal examples privately to the principal and assure the students that their comments will be kept confidential.

❖ Invite the individual student and his parent[s] in for a conference and explain the teacher's concerns. Ask directly what the teacher and the school have been missing and what the student needs in order to reach his potential in this particular class.

Scenario No. 3

The school counselor was growing more and more frustrated because Joey would not tell her with whom he lived. When asked if his father lived with him, he evaded the question and wouldn't reply. She asked another colleague for support and they continued to prod Joey about his home life, but he remained resistant. When they reported their lack of information to the literacy director, she, an African American woman, shared that the boy may have been told by his mother not to share who lived in the home. She realized the other women were unaware of how the welfare system worked. The white women responded by saying, "How do you know things like that?" The white women were frustrated; the black woman was frustrated the women were ignorant of the systems under which their children lived.

Questions:

1. What prompted the counselor to ask the question?

2. Why did she feel it was necessary to bring a colleague into the situation? Was there an impending crisis which would justify breaching counselor and student client confidentiality?

Considerations:

Realizing that the African American literacy director probably recognized correctly that Joey was protective of his family's financial situation, it is imperative that no one make assumptions about any student without verification or validation by the student, his or her family, or the official record. In many instances, information such as this may be none of the school's concern.

There are many reasons children keep family business within the family. Financial reasons are among them. Unconventional family configurations are another. Blended or extended families, unmarried parents, gay or lesbian parents, undocumented families, illness, or a family member who is or has been incarcerated are just a few of the reasons children and adolescents feel protective of their families.

Pushing a child to disclose anything rarely helps and often hinders. If there is a piece of information necessary to the student's schooling, it probably is somewhere in the student's file or it can be obtained in other ways.

Interventions:

❖ Consider the real reason this question arose. Say it out loud to a trusted professional friend. Try saying, "I need to know _____, because _____."

❖ If the information is critical, first tell the child why you need to know. Perhaps he can find a way to give the information without divulging private family business or causing himself embarrassment or shame.

❖ Always thank your student for the information they do share. When children talk about themselves, it is a gift of trust and respect. Never take any small piece of information for granted.

Wholistic Reflection Worksheet

I think _____

_____

(What my mind tells me about this person, event, situation, or problem.)

I feel _____

_____

(The emotions I feel and the physical sensations I have in my body in response to this situation.)

I know _____

_____

(Considering my thoughts and feelings, what facts have I concluded.)

I believe _____

_____

(What does my intuition or faith tell me in regard to this person, event, situation, or problem.)

Cultural Consideration Event Summary   Date _____

Description of Event

_____

_____

_____

_____

_____

My First Thoughts _____

My Body Felt _____

I Knew _____

I Believed _____

What I Wanted to Do _____

What I Did _____

Result _____

What I Will Do Next Time

_____

_____

How I Feel About How I Handled Things

_____

_____

_____

Personal Rights

The Right to Promote One's Own Dignity and Self Respect
The Right to be Treated with Respect by Others
The Right to Say "No"
The Right to Experience and Express One's Feelings
The Right to Take Time to Think before Acting
The Right to Change One's Mind
The Right to Ask for What One Wants
The Right to Achieve Less than is Humanly Possible
The Right to Ask for Information
The Right to Make Mistakes
The Right to Feel Good About One's Self

Cultural Self-Awareness Matrix

History & Historic Memory   Geography & Regional Origins

Circumstances & Situation   Affinity & Relational Bonds

156

Feelings/Emotions

Happy

Excited	Understood	Silly	Loved	Proud
Grateful	Relieved	Friendly	Comfortable	

Sad

Depressed	Misunderstood	Worried	Bored	Grief
Lonely	Sorry	Hurt	Disappointed	

Angry

Mad	Cranky	Cheated	Vengeful	Violent
Upset	Insulted	Jealous	Disgusted	

Scared

Nervous	Fearful	Shy	Suspicious	Bullied
Frightened	Jumpy	Shocked	Intimidated	

Confused	Different	Embarrassed	Guilty	Shame	Numb

Body Signals

Tired, Exhausted, Numb

Tense, Tight, Teeth Clinched or Grinding

Anxious, Jittery

Joint or Muscle Pain, Achy, Hurt

Stomach Trouble, Nauseous, Diarrhea, Stomach Pain

Dizziness, Fuzzy, Light-headed, Spacey

Funny, Weird, Skin Crawling, Tingly

Flashbacks, Body Memories; Intrusive Thoughts, Beliefs, or Voices

Can't Sleep, Bad Dreams, Sleep too Much

Hungry, Cravings, Empty

Satisfied, Full, Too Full

Strong, Beautiful, Energetic

Rules of Engagement

Arrive Unencumbered

Enter with Intent

Attend to Self-Care

Respect Others

Circulate

Ask Questions

Leave Satisfied

138

Guidelines for Clear Communication

Clear communication includes

- Respect of one another
- Being honest
- Speaking one at a time and allowing equal time
- "I" statements
- Clarifying by repeating
- Giving reasons
- Making compromises
- Admitting mistakes
- Time-outs and taking breaks
- Observing the guidelines agreed upon

Clear communication does *not* include

- Name calling
- Generalizations
- "You" statements
- Tangents
- Violence, threats, or intimidation
- Changing the rules
- Expecting a winner and loser
- Expecting a right or wrong
- Saving up issues and dumping them all at once
- Mind reading
- Assumptions
- Denying the facts
- Gloating over a victory
- Stonewalling or ignoring the other person

Barriers to communication include

- Habit
- Fear of displeasing someone
- Mistaken sense of responsibility
- Protecting the other person
- Guilt and/or shame
- Misinformation about personal rights
- Reluctance to give up benefits of silence
- Financial insecurity
- Chemical abuse or dependency
- Abuse or violence
- Secrets

Causes of poor communication are

- Anger
- Depression
- Misinformation/ignorance
- Feelings of vulnerability
- Lack of empathy for the other person
- Mistrust of the other person
- Control feels good

Additional communication considerations:

- Facial Expressions
- Gestures
- Touch
- Interrupting
- Tone and volume of voice
- Control over space

Conflict Resolution

- Deal with one issue at a time.

- Set a time limit.

- Follow the guidelines for clear communication and rigidly abide by them.

- Stay current. Do not talk about past problems unless they directly relate to the present.

- Allow both talking and listening time.

- Do not interrupt.

- Arrive at a solution good for both parties. A problem has not been solved if someone has to "give in" for the sake of ending a conflict.

Problem Solving Steps

1. Define the problem.

2. Specify the desired outcome.

3. List ways to attain the goal.

4. Narrow the focus to the top three choices.

5. List positives and negatives of each choice.

6. Calculate findings.

7. If things remain unclear, re-examine the problem definition and desired outcomes. It may be that the core issue[s] have not been stated clearly.

Resources

Amnesty International	www.amnesty.org
The Equity Alliance	www.equityallianceatasu.org
Human Rights Watch	www.hrw.org
International Institute	www.iistl.org
National Association for Multicultural Education	www.nameorg.org
National Center for Cultural Competence	www.nccc.georgetown.edu/index.html
Southern Poverty Law Center	www.splcenter.org
Teaching Tolerance	www.tolerance.org
The White Privilege Conference	www.whiteprivilegeconference.com
Anti-Defamation League	www.adl.org

Ontario Consultants on
Religious Tolerance
Box 27026
Kingston, Ontario Canada K7M
8W5
PO Box 128
Watertown, NY 13601–0128
Fax (613) 547–9015
www.religioustolerance.org

The PJ Library   www.pjlibrary.org

Disability Resources   www.disabilityresources.org

Disability Rights, Education, &   www.dredf.org
Defense Fund

National Institutes of Health
(NIH)
9000 Rockville Pike
Bethesda, MD 20892
www.nih.gov

National Alliance of Mental
Illness
3803 N. Fairfax Drive, Suite 100
Arlington, VA 22203
(703) 524-7600
Fax: (703) 524-9094
www.nami.org

Child Welfare Information
Gateway
Children's Bureau/ACYF
1250 Maryland Avenue, SW,
Eighth Floor
Washington, DC 20024
(800) 394-3366
www.childwelfare.gov

The Ophelia Project   www.opheliaproject.org

American Association of   www.aauw.org
University Women

Expanding Your Horizons   www.expandingyourhorizons
                                        .org

*Family Outing: A Guide to the Coming-Out Process for Gays, Lesbians,
and Their Families*
Authors Chastity Bono and Billie Fitzpatrick, Little, Brown, &
Company, 1999

My Princess Boy
Cheryl Kilodavis, KD Talent, LLC, 2010

And Tango Makes Three
Authors Justin Richardson and Peter Parnell, Simon & Schuster,
2005

Girls Inc.   www.girlsinc.org

GLSEN, the Gay, Lesbian and   www.glsen.org
Straight Education Network

LAMBDA   www.lambda.org

National Center for Lesbian   www.nclrights.org
Rights

National Abstinence Education   www.abstinenceassociation.org
Association

New Moon Magazine   www.newmoon.com

Parents and Friends of Lesbians   www.pflag.org
and Gays

Planned Parenthood   www.plannedparenthood.org

Real Boys' Voices, William Pollack, Random House, 2000

Tough Guise: Violence, Media, and Crisis of Masculinity (Video)
Media Education Foundation www.mediaed.org

*Why Boys Don't Talk and Why We Care: A Mother's Guide to
Connection*
Authors Susan Morris Shaffer and Linda Perlman Gordon

Rosalind Wiseman   www.rosalindwiseman.com
Author of *Queen Bees and
Wannabes*

Mid-Atlantic Equity   www.maec.org
Consortium, 2000

Women's Educational Equity   www.edc.org/womensequity
Act

National Network of
Partnership Schools
Johns Hopkins University
3003 N. Charles Street, Suite 200
Baltimore, MD 21218
(410) 516–8800
Fax: (410) 516–8890
www.csos.jhu.edu/p2000/
center.htm

National Parent Teacher
Organizations
541 N Fairbanks Court
Suite 1300
Chicago, IL 60611–3396
(312) 670–6782
Toll-Free: (800) 307–4PTA (4782)
Fax: (312) 670–6783
www.pta.org

National Service Learning   www.service
Partnership   -learningpartnership.org

National Service Resource
Center
ETR Associates
4 Carbonero Way
Scotts Valley, CA 95066
(800) 860-2684 or (831) 438-4060
TTY: (831) 461-0205
www.nationalserviceresources
.org

Association for Supervision and   www.ascd.org
Curriculum Development

National Staff Development   www.nsdc.org
Council

Educating for Change   www.educatingforchange.com

Band Shades: Multicultural   www.bandshades.com
Bandages

Diversity Tool Kit   www.diversity.aclin.org

Enchanted Learning   www.enchantedlearning.com

The Multicultural Toy Box   www.multiculturaltoybox.com

The Artist's Way
Author Julia Cameron, Jeremy
P. Tarcher/Penguin, 2002

*Between Therapists: The Processing
of Transference and
Countertransference Material*
Author Arthur Robbins, Jessica
Kingsley Publishers, 1988

*Walking in This World: The
Practical Art of Creativity*
Author Julia Cameron, Jeremy
P. Tarcher/Penguin, 2003

References

Abrams, L. S., & Gibson, P. (2007). Reframing multicultural education: Teaching white privilege in the social work curriculum. *Journal of Social Work Education, 43,* 147–160.

Adams, M., Bell, L., & Griffin, P. (2006). *Teaching for diversity and social justice: A sourcebook* (2nd ed.). New York, NY: Routledge.

Agarwal, R., Epstein, S., Oppenheim, R., Oyler, C., & Sonu, D. (2010). From ideal to practice and back again: Beginning teachers teaching for social justice. *Journal of Teacher Education, 61*(3), 237–247.

American Psychological Association. (2001). *Publication Manual of the American Psychological Association* (5th ed.). Washington, DC: Author.

Anderson, K. L. (1996). Gangs, Cults and Mind Control. *Counseling Children and Adolescence,* St. Louis, Missouri.

Anderson, K. (2002). Full circle: Countertransference containment through mandala making. Final project, St. Louis Institute of Art Psychotherapy. St. Louis, MO: Self.

Anderson, K. L. (1996, 1999, 2001, 2012). Inward bound: A wholistic roadmap for wellness. St. Louis, MO.

Anderson, K. L. (1998/2007). Meal of the imagination: Breaking bread, breaking down barriers. *Workshop Series.* St. Louis, MO.

Anderson, K. L. (2010a). Cultural self-awareness matrix. *Culturally Considerate Practice.* St. Louis, MO: MabelMedia.

Anderson, K. L. (2010b). *Culturally considerate school counseling: Helping without bias.* Thousand Oaks, CA: Corwin.

Anderson, K. L., & Davis, B. M. (2010). *Creating culturally considerate schools: Educating without bias.* St. Louis, MO: Educating for Change.

Banks, C., & Banks, J. (1995). Equity pedagogy: An essential component of multicultural education. *Theory Into Practice, 43*(3), 152–158.

Banks, J. A., & McGee Banks, C. A. (2001). *Handbook of research on multicultural education.* San Francisco: Jossey-Bass.

Banks, J. A., & McGee Banks, C. A. (2009). *Multicultural education: Issues and perspectives* (7th ed.). New York: Wiley.

Beck, A. T. (1979). *Cognitive treatment and the emotional disorders.* New York, NY: Penguin Books.

Bennett, M. J. (1993). Towards ethnorelativism: A developmental model of intercultural sensitivity. In R. M. Paige (Ed.), *Education for the Intercultural Experience* (pp. 21–71). Yarmouth, ME: Intercultural Press.

Berlak, A., & Moyenda, S. (2001). *Taking it personally: Racism in the classroom from kindergarten to college.* Philadelphia, PA: Temple University Press.

Bickmore, K. (1999). Elementary curriculum about conflict resolution: Can children handle global politics? *Theory and Research in Social Education, 27*(1), 45–69.

Bloom, L. (2008). *The art of apology: How to apologize effectively to almost anyone.* USA: Green Angel Media, LLC.

Britzman, D. (2000, May/June). Teacher education in the confusion of our times. *Journal of Teacher Education, 51*(3), 200–205.

Brown, L. (1989). New voices, new visions: Toward a Lesbian/Gay paradigm for psychology. *Psychology of Women Quarterly, 13,* 445–458.

Bueller, J., Gere, A., Dallavis, C., & Havilland, V. S. (2009). Normalizing the fraughtness: How emotion, race, and school context complicated cultural competence. *Journal of Teacher Education, 60*(4), 408–418.

Burris, C., & Garrity, D. (2011). *Opening the common core: How to bring all students to college and career readiness.* Thousand Oaks, CA: Corwin.

Cameron, J. (2002). *The Artist's Way.* New York, NY: Tarcher.

Camilleri, V. A. (Ed.). (2007). *Healing the inner city child: Creative arts therapy with at-risk youth.* Philadelphia: Jessica Kingsley Publishers.

Cochran-Smith, M. (2004). *Walking the road: Race, diversity, and social justice in teacher education.* New York, NY: Teachers College.

Common Core State Standards Initiative. (2011, November). *Mission Statement.* Retrieved from www.corestandards.org

Cordova, R. A., & Matthiesen, A. L. (2010, March). Reading, writing, and mapping our worlds into being: Shared teacher inquiries into whose literacies count. *The Reading Teacher, 63*(6), 452–464.

Council on Social Work Education. (2005, February). *Educational policy and accreditation standards.* Alexandria, VA: Author.

Crenshaw, K. (1989). Demarginalizing the intersection of race and sex: A Black feminist critique of antidiscrimination doctrine, feminist theory, and antiracist politics. *University of Chicago Legal Forum, 1989,* 139–167.

Crenshaw, K. (1991, July). Mapping the margins: Intersectionality, identity politics, and violence against women of color. *Stanford Law Review, 43*(1241), 1241–1299.

Crenshaw, K. (1992). Whose story is it, anyway? Feminist and antiracist appropriations of Anita Hill. In T. Morrison (Ed.), *Race-ing justice, engendering power* (pp. 402–440). New York, NY: Pantheon Books.

Crocco, M. S., & Costigan, A. T. (2007). The narrowing of the curriculum and pedagogy in the age of accountability: Urban educators speak out. *Urban Education, 42*(6), 512–513.

Darling-Hammond, L. (2010). *The flat world and education: How America's commitment to equity will determine our future.* New York, NY: Teachers College Press.

Darling-Hammond, L., French, J., & Garcia-Lopez, S. P. (2002). *Learning to teach for social justice.* New York, NY: Teachers College Press.

Davis, B. M. (2006). *How to teach students who don't look like you: Culturally relevant teaching strategies.* Thousand Oaks, CA: Corwin.

Derman-Sparks, L., & Ramsey, P. (2006). *What if all the kids are white? Anti-bias, multicultural education with young children and families.* New York, NY: Teachers College Press.

Effrem, K. R. (2010, April 7). Testimony Regarding the Common Core Standards Initiative. [Testimony, U.S. House of Representatives]. Washington, DC: EdWatch.

Ellis, A. (1978) *Growth through reason: Verbatim cases in rational-emotive therapy.* Chatsworth, CA: M. Powers.

Essed, P. (1990). *Everyday racism: Reports from women of two cultures.* Claremont, CA: Hunter House.

Essed, P. (2002). Everyday racism: A new approach to the study of racism. In P. Essed & D. T. Goldberg (Eds.), *Race critical theories: Text and context* (pp. 176–194). Malden, MA: Basil Blackwell.

Feiman-Nemser, S. (2003). What new teachers need to learn. *Educational Leadership, 60*(8), 25–29.

Fine, M. (1997). Witnessing whiteness. In M. Fines, L. Weis, L. Powell, & L. Wong, *Off white: Readings on race and power in society* (pp. 57–65). New York, NY: Routledge.

Frankenberg, R. (1993). *The Social construction of whiteness: White women, race matters.* Minneapolis, MN: University of Minnesota Press.

Frankenberg, R. (1997). *Displacing whiteness.* Durham, NC: Duke University Press.

French, J. R. P., Jr., & Raven, B. The bases of power. In D. Cartwright (Ed.), *Studies in social power.* Ann Arbor: University of Michigan Press, 1959.

Freud, A. (1974). Four lectures on psychoanalysis for teachers and parents. In *The writings of Anna Freud, Volume 1 1922–1935* (pp. 73–90). New York: International Universities Press. (Original work published in 1930)

Galman, S., Pica-Smith, C., & Rosenberger, C. (2010). Aggressive and tender navigations: Teacher educators confront whiteness in their practice. *Journal of Teacher Education, 61*(3), 225–236.

Gardner, H. (1983). *Frames of mind: The theory of multiple intelligences* (10th ed.). New York, NY: Basic Books.

Gardner, M. R. (1999). The true teacher and the furor to teach. In S. Appel (Ed.), *Psychoanalysis and Pedagogy* (pp. 93–102). Westport, CT: Bergin & Garvey.

Gay, G. (2001). *Handbook of research on multicultural education.* (J. A. Banks, & C. A. McGee Banks, Eds.) San Francisco, CA: Jossey-Bass.

Gay, G. (2002, March/April). Preparing for culturally responsive teaching. *Journal of Teacher Education, 53*(2), 106–116.

Gay, G. (2010). *Culturally responsive teaching: Theory, research, and practice* (2nd ed.). New York, NY: Teachers College Press.

Gehlbach, H. (2010). The social side of school: Why teachers need social psychology. *Educational Psychology Review, 22*(3), 349–362.

Gibbons, K. (2010). Circle Justice: A creative arts approach to conflict resolution in the classroom. *Art Therapy: Journal of the American Art Therapy Association, 27*(2), 84–89.

Gillespie, D., Ashbaugh, L., & DeFiore, J. (2002). White women teaching white women about white privilege, race cognizance, and social action: Toward a pedagogical pragmatics. *Race, Ethnicity, and Education, 5*(3), 237–253.

Glassi, J. P., & Akos, P. (2007). *Strengths-based school counseling: Promoting student development and achievement.* MahWah, NJ: Erlbaum.

Goldner, V. (1988). Generation and gender: Normative and covert hierarchies. *Family Process, 27,* 18–31.

Grof, C. (1993). *The thirst for wholeness: Attachment, addiction, and the spiritual path.* New York, NY: HarperCollins.

Hale-Benson, J. E., & Hilliard, A. G., III. (1986). *Black children: Their roots, culture, and learning styles.* Baltimore, MD: The Johns Hopkins University Press.

Hehir, T. (2002). Eliminating ableism in education. *Harvard Educational Review, 72*(1), 1–32.

Helms, J. E. (Ed.). (1990). *Black and white perspectives on racial identity: Theory, research, and practices.* Westport, CT: Greenwood.

Helms, J. E. (1995). An update of Helm's White and People of Color racial identity models. In J. G. Ponterotto, L. P. Casas, P. Suzuki, & C. M. Alexander, *Handbook of multicultural education* (pp. 181–197). Thousand Oaks, CA: Sage.

Hirschman, P. (2006). *Get to work: A manifesto for women of the world.* New York, NY: Penguin Group.

Hodges, J. (1995). *Conflict resolution for the young child.* Retrieved from ERIC database. (ED394624).

Hollins, E., & Guzman, M. T. (2005). *Research on preparing teachers for diverse populations.* AERA Panel on Research and Teacher Education. Mahwah, NJ: Erlbaum.

hooks, b. (2004). *The will to change: Men, masculinity, and love.* New York, NY: Atria Books.

Hughes, C., Newkirk, R., & Stenhjem, P. H. (2010). Addressing the challenge of disfranchisement of youth: Poverty and racism in schools. *Reclaiming Children and Youth, 19*(1), 22–26.

Irvine, J. J. (2003). *Educating teachers for diversity: Seeing with the cultural eye.* New York, NY: Teachers College Press.

Jensen, E. (2005). *Teaching with brain in mind* (2nd ed.). Alexandria, VA: Association for Supervision and Curriculum Development.

Jung, C. G. (1971). *Psychological types* (A revision by R. F. C. Hull of the translation by H. G. Baynes). Princeton, NJ: Princeton University Press. (Original work published in German 1921)

Kluth, P., Straut, D., & Biklen, D. (2003). *Access to academics for all students: Critical approaches to inclusive curriculum, instruction, and policy.* Mahwah, NJ: Erlbaum.

Knudson, S. V. (2005). Intersectionality: A theoretical inspiration in the analysis of minority cultures and identities in textbooks. *Eighth International Conference on Learning and Educational Media,* (pp. 61–76). Caen, France.

Kumashiro, K. (2004). *Against common sense: Teaching and learning toward social justice.* New York, NY: RoutledgeFalmer.

Lachat, M. A. (1999). *Standards, equity, and cultural diversity.* Providence, RI: The Education Alliance, Brown University.

Ladson-Billings, G. (1994). *The dreamkeepers: Successful teachers of African American children.* San Francisco, CA: Jossey-Bass.

Lea, V. (2004). The reflective cultural portfolio: Identifying public cultural scripts in the private voices of white student teachers. *Journal of Teacher Education, 55*(2), 116–127.

Lindsey, R. B. (2004). *The culturally proficient school: An implementation guide for school leaders.* Thousand Oaks, CA: Corwin.

Lindsey, R., Roberts, L. M., & CampbellJones, F. (2005). *The culturally proficient school: An implementation guide for school leaders.* Thousand Oaks, CA: Corwin.

Linton, S. (1998). *Claiming disability: Knowledge and identity.* New York: New York University Press.

Lucas, S. (2008). Constructing colorblind classrooms. In M. Pollock, *Everyday antiracism: Getting real about race in school* (pp. 62–66). New York, NY: New Press.

Marx, S. (2004). Regarding whiteness: Exploring and intervening in the effects of white racism in teacher education. *Equity and Excellence in Education, 37*(1), 1–113.

Marzano, R. J., & Pickering, D. J. (2011). *The highly engaged classroom.* Bloomington, IN: Marzano Research Laboratory.

McIntosh, P. (1988). White privilege and male privilege: A personal account of coming to see correspondences through work in women's studies. *Working Paper No. 189.* Wellesley, MA: Wellesley College Center for Research on Women.

McIntosh, P. (1989). White privilege: Unpacking the invisible knapsack. *Peace and Freedom, July/August,* 10–12.

McLeod, J. (2010). *Case study research in counseling and psychotherapy.* Thousand Oaks, CA: Sage.

Menkel-Meadow, C. (2000). Telling stories in school: Using case studies and stories to teach legal ethics. *Fordham Law Review, 69,* 787.

Moore, B. E., & Fine, B. D. (Eds.). (1990). *Psychoanalytic terms and concepts.* New Haven, CT: Yale University Press and the American Psychoanalytic Association.

Nash, J. (2008). Re-thinking intersectionality. *Feminist Review, 89,* 2–15.

National Immigration Law Center. (2011). *DREAM Act: Summary.* Los Angeles, CA: National Immigration Law Center.

Nieto, S. (2005). Public education in the twentieth century and beyond: High hopes, broken promises, and uncertain future. *Harvard Educational Review, 75*(1), 43–64.

Piaget, J. (1951). *The biological problem of intelligence: Organization and pathology of thought.* New York, NY: Columbia University Press.

Pinderhughes, E. (1989). *Understanding race, ethnicity, & power: The key to efficacy in clinical practice.* New York, NY: The Free Press.

Pollock, M., Deckman, S., Mira, M., & Shalaby, C. (2010, December). But what can I do? Three necessary tensions in teaching teachers about race. *Journal of Teacher Education, 61*(3), 211–224.

Ponterotto, J. G., Utsey, S. O., & Pedersen, P. B. (2006). *Preventing prejudice: A guide for counselors, educators, and parents* (2nd ed.). Thousand Oaks, CA: Sage.

Ravitch, D. (2010). *The death and life of the great American school system.* New York, NY: Basic Books.

Ravitch, S. M. (2006). *School counseling principles: Multiculturalism and diversity.* Alexandria, VA: American School Counselor Association.

Reamer, F. G. (2009). *The social work ethics casebook: Cases and commentary.* Washington, DC: NASW Press.

Relevant Strategies. (2011). *Bias and sensitivity review of the common core state standards in English language arts and mathematics: Implementation recommendations report.* Olympia: Washington Superintendent of Public Instruction.

Rhee, M. (2010, December 13). "What I've learned." *Newsweek,* pp. 36–41.

Rivers, J. L. (2011). *Common Core Standards and assessments.* Washington, DC: League of Women Voters.

Romano, P. (2009, June). *Commemorating the past: An introduction to the study of historical memory.* Retrieved from http://greensborotrc.org/intro.doc.

Roth, S. (1989). Psychotherapy with lesbian couples: Individual issues, female socialization, and the social context. In M. McGoldrick, C. Anderson, & F. Walsh, *Women in families: A framework for family therapy* (pp. 286–307). New York, NY: W. W. Norton & Company.

Rundstrom Williams, T. (2009). The reflective model of intercultural competency: A multidimensional, qualitative approach to study abroad assessment. *Frontiers: The Interdisciplinary Journal of Study Abroad, XVIII*(Fall), 289–306.

Rutstein, N. (2001). *The racial conditioning of our children: Ending psychological genocide in schools.* Albion, MI: National Resource Center for the Healing of Racism.

Saleebey, D. (1994). Culture, theory, and narrative: The intersection of meanings in practice. *Social Work, 39,* 351–359.

Sapon-Shevin, M. (1999). *Because we can change the world: A practical guide to building cooperative, inclusive, classroom communities.* Needham Heights, MA: Allyn & Bacon.

Singleton, G. E., & Linton, C. (2006). *Courageous conversations about race: A field guild for achieving equity in schools.* Thousand Oaks, CA: Corwin.

Sink, C. (2010, April). Commentary: Critical reflections on the ethical and professional considerations in writing about clients. *Counseling and Values, 54,* 157–166.

Sleeter, C. (2000/2001, Winter). Diversity vs. white privilege. (Rethinking Schools, Interviewer)

Sleeter, C. (2001a). *Handbook of research on multicultural education.* (J. A. Banks, & C. A. McGee Banks, Eds.) San Francisco: Jossey-Bass.

Sleeter, C. E. (2001b, March/April). Preparing Teachers for Culturally Diverse Schools: Research and the Overwhelming Presence of Whiteness. *Journal of Teacher Education, 52*(2), 96–106.

Sleeter, C. E., & Delgado Bernal, D. (2004). Critical pedagogy, critical race theory, and antiracist education: Their implications for multicultural education. In J. A. Banks & C. M. Banks (Eds.), *Handbook of Research on Multicultural Education* (2nd ed.; pp. 240–260). Jossey Bass.

Solomon, R. P., Portelli, J. P., Daniel, B.-J., & Campbell, A. (2005, July). The discourse of denial: How white teacher candidates construct race, racism and "white privilege." *Race, Ethnicity, and Education, 8*(2), 147–169.

Sontag, S. (1977). *On photography.* New York: Picador USA.

Sousa, D. A. (1998, December 16). Is the fuss about brain research justified? *Education Week, 18*(16), pp. 35, 52.

Sousa, D. A. (2006). *How the brain learns* (3rd ed.). Thousand Oaks, CA: Corwin.

Sperry, L. (2010, April). Writing about clients: An overview of ethical and professional issues in clinical case reports. *Counseling and Values, 54,* 83–87.

Sperry, L., & Pies, R. (2010). Writing about clients: Ethical considerations and options. *Counseling and Values, 54,* 88–94.

State Board of Education Academic Standards Committee. (2011). *Implementating the Common Core Standards in Pennsylvania: Reflections from the field; A State Board of Education White Paper.* Pennsylvania Dept. of Education, Academic Standards Committee. Harrisburg: Pennsylvania Department of Education.

Straus, V. (2010, March 10). The problem(s) with the Common Core Standards. *The Washington Post.*

Sue, D. W., & Sue, D. (1999). *Counseling the culturally different* (3rd ed.). New York: Wiley.

Sue, D. W., & Sue, D. (2008). *Counseling the culturally diverse: Theory and practice* (5th ed.). Hoboken, NJ: Wiley.

Tieman, J. S. (2007). The ghost in the schoolroom: A primer in the lessons of shame. *Schools, 4*(2), 39–55.

U.S. Department of Education. (2010, April 9). Overview information: Race to the Top Fund assessment program: Notice inviting applicants for new awards for Fiscal Year (FYI) 2010. *Federal Register.* Washington, DC: United States Government.

Venson, R. S. (2008). *Messengers of peace: Facilitators' guide.* Unpublished manuscript.

Waldegrave, C., & Tamasese, K. (1993). Some central ideas in the 'Just Therapy' approach. *Australian & New Zealand Journal of Family Therapy, 5*(2), 1–8.

Walker, A. (1992). *Possessing the secret of joy.* New York, NY: Pocket Books.

Walters, M., Carter, B., Papp, P., & Silverstein, O. (1988). *The invisible web, gender patterns in family relationships.* New York, NY: Guilford Press.

Watts-Jones, D. (2010). Location of the self: Opening the door to dialogue on intersectionality in the therapy process. *Family Process, 49*(5), 405–420.

Wolfe, P. (2010). *Brain matters: Translating research into classroom practice* (2nd ed.). Alexandria, VA: Association for Supervision and Curriculum Development.

Zeichner, K. M. (1992). *Educating teachers for cultural diversity.* East Lansing, MI: National Center for Research on Teacher Learning.

Index

CORWIN
A SAGE Company

The Corwin logo—a raven striding across an open book—represents the union of courage and learning. Corwin is committed to improving education for all learners by publishing books and other professional development resources for those serving the field of PreK–12 education. By providing practical, hands-on materials, Corwin continues to carry out the promise of its motto: **"Helping Educators Do Their Work Better."**